BullyProof

As Royal Air Force Aircrew, having an Alpha personality was part of the selection process. Operating alongside, and communicating with Alpha type personalities to provide a conducive and positive result to a common objective, takes a cognitive and purposeful approach. When it's done successively the results are fantastic, however, when done within a corrosive environment with a lack of skill and knowledge of the approach, the results can be disastrous. *BullyProof* will supply those new to this communication style the skills required to maintain a positive outcome when dealing with Alpha personalities. For those trained and experienced in leadership and soft skills, *BullyProof* will provide additional tools for the leadership toolbox. A must read when dealing with Alpha personalities amongst a new generation.

Martin Naylor, Former Royal Air Force Aircrew and IT leader at Raymond James

Rob has a natural ability to make complex theories both accessible and practical for easy application within our day-to-day lives. *BullyProof* builds on both Simple is the New Smart and Rob's extensive professional experience to hit all the marks.

Eric D. McCollum, MD, MPH Associate Professor, Department of Pediatrics, Johns Hopkins School of Medicine

The abuse and misuse of power have long been problems in the institutions we inhabit. Despite this being the case, there have been very little prescriptive resources to combat bullying.

Fazio changes that by taking us through a psychological framework that allows us to recognize bullying in ourselves as well as the environments around us. With his framework, perhaps we truly will be able to *BullyProof* our society.

Tayo Rockson - Author of *Use Your Difference To Make A Difference*

In this amazing book, Dr. Rob Fazio demonstrates that no matter how dysfunctional the behavior of toxic "Alpha" people are in our lives—at the workplace or at home—we have power to self-coach ourselves to mitigate and even reverse the damage. Given his experiences and research, *BullyProof* offers the reader a host of compelling strategies. One of them "H.O.W." is designed to help us understand habits, obstacles, and most importantly, how to create a way forward. Regardless of your current situation, this valuable book is just the ticket to empower and protect you from needless struggle. If you're looking for a hands-on road map for taking charge of your life and circumstances, this is it. No ifs, ands, or buts!

Joseph Luciani, Ph.D.
International bestselling author of *Self-Coaching*

Bullying—in the workplace, in the political arena, in relationships—is on the rise, a product of our global stress and uncertainty unbalancing and overwhelming our ability to cope and perform. Combine that with out-moded ideas about driving performance and "do more with less" environments, sprinkled with a touch of emotional tone-deafness, and voila, bullies are born. And, as Rob Fazio points out in his new book, *BullyProof,* because so often bullying pays off, at least in the short-term, with faster results. The residual human and financial cost, to the bullied and to the organizations that tolerate bullying, however, is enormous.

If you have ever been bullied and want to know how to respond more effectively, or if you suspect that you yourself may be resorting to bullying and want to fix that, this book is for you. Packed with stories from a variety of high-performance domains, *BullyProof* takes you from theory to practice with specific strategies and tools. You will understand, learn, and be to equipped to respond – to yourself, those key relationships, and through to an organizational level – to achieve better outcomes even in high pressure situations with less human suffering and collateral damage. The world needs this book more than ever right now and I'm glad Rob Fazio wrote it.

Kirsten Peterson, PhD, Performance Psychologist at Kirsten Peterson Consulting and Former Senior Sport Psychologist at the United States Olympic Committee

An insightful journey that activates its readers into putting learning to action.

Talapady Srivatsa Bhat, Engineering Manager at Samsung

As a sales executive who has run sales teams of 100+ and smaller teams as well, one thing that is always a challenge is being able to communicate effectively and keeping the team motivated. During my tenure, I have had the unfortunate responsibility of managing aggressive, condescending and dominant sales people and managers and I wish *BullyProof* was around to help guide my communication. Rob's guidance on developing Value Based Power and leveraging your Subtle Strength has helped how I think about managing tough employees while refining how I think about my communication and approach with clients. Rob helped me think about how I can better engage and influence people through Motivational Currency and truly understand what motivates and drives behaviors of my sales team. What an outstanding opportunity to learn and grow both personally and professionally. I can't advocate enough for *BullyProof* and what it has done for me as a sales leader.

David Gensler, Chief Revenue Officer, Basis Technologies

In a world where we need more kindness, allyship and positivity, *BullyProof* offers sound and applicable advice on how to manage stressful dynamics while offering empathy and strength. *BullyProof* gives the answer to the question, how do I own my power and authenticity and encourage others to do the same. Rob Fazio a guide to creating strength out of stress.

Barb Cowan, Vice President Talent and Inclusion
Comcast Advertising at Comcast

BULLY PROOF

Using Subtle Strength
to Influence Alphas
and Strengthen Society

ROB FAZIO, *PhD*

NEW YORK

LONDON • NASHVILLE • MELBOURNE • VANCOUVER

BULLY*PROOF*

Using Subtle Strength to Influence Alphas and Strengthen Society

Published in New York, New York, by Morgan James Publishing. Morgan James is a trademark of Morgan James, LLC. www.MorganJamesPublishing.com

Proudly distributed by Ingram Publisher Services.

ISBN 9781631957444 paperback
ISBN 9781631959332 case laminate
ISBN 9781631957451 ebook
Library of Congress Control Number:
2021917021

Cover Design by:
Rachel Lopez
www.r2cdesign.com

Interior Design by:
Chris Treccani
www.3dogcreative.net

Jacket Author Photo by:
Mary Mcilvaine
www.marymcilvaine.com/

Morgan James is a proud partner of Habitat for Humanity Peninsula and Greater Williamsburg. Partners in building since 2006.

Get involved today! Visit MorganJamesPublishing.com/giving-back

*To the alphas I love and learn from, my wife Keli
and daughters Reese and Rae.*

We're Kind, We're Strong, and We Help People.

*And to Dad. If you were around today, you'd be
the second person in line to buy a copy. The first person
would be the one that got ahead because you were kind
enough to Hold the Door.*

Thank you. 143.

CONTENTS

INTRODUCTION
Be the Robin Hood of Power

None of us can control where we grow up, but all of us can control how we show up. I am grateful I grew up in Bergen County, New Jersey. I had everything a kid could want. The area provided me with many opportunities and important life lessons. My grandparents and cousins lived in Queens and visiting them allowed me to meet people from all walks of life. My dad worked as a senior executive in downtown New York City. He grew up in the Bronx with very few resources, and his dedication to his family and friends and his desire to be a good boss opened many doors.

My dad also worked for a power-hungry, manipulative CFO. I remember countless times seeing the anxiety in my dad's face when he got home from work. He commuted two hours each way into downtown NYC and was determined to be a family man. He was always there to be a dad and created a childhood I am grateful for.

Then he was suddenly laid off after twenty-six years as a senior executive. I wasn't used to seeing concern about the future in my parents' eyes. The vision of my mom washing out plastic sandwich bags so we could reuse them is still with me every day.

At forty-five, my dad got a quadruple bypass and was never the same. I know genetics play a significant role, but I believe the dysfunction in his work environment contributed to his heart disease.

My experience growing up with two loving parents was still overwhelmingly positive, and my father went on to be a successful executive and never had ill will toward people who treated him poorly. But I had now been introduced to what it felt like when other people were dealing your hand in life. I didn't like how it felt, nor did I like seeing my mother and father deal with the financial and emotional pressure of having three children. During this time, it felt as if our lives were not in our control, and I wanted to find a way to change that.

I didn't know it at the time, but I became obsessed with power and influence. I didn't want other people to have my dad's experience working for a dysfunctional boss. I also began to take responsibility for how I responded to setbacks. I was someone who worried about everything, which led to me talking myself out of many opportunities. When it came to sports, I was convinced I wasn't going to be good enough, fast enough, or athletic enough. When it came to school, I was convinced I wasn't smart enough and tended to give up the moment learning became too difficult. I struggled with reading comprehension and understanding complex information and still do to this day.

I was determined not to live my life feeling afraid, weak, and powerless, so I set out to learn about confidence and mental toughness. As I mentioned, I wasn't a good student. I didn't even want to go to college, but my parents believed in me enough to push me to grow. The friends I met at Pace University in New York taught me how to speak up, enjoy life, and look out for people. Although I had no interest in college at first, something clicked and I worked hard to transfer to Penn State. At Penn State, my mother suggested I combine two things I loved: sport and psychology. We were watching the Olympics when the story broke about Nancy Kerrigan and Tonya Harding. My mom had heard that Nancy Kerrigan was seeing a sport psychologist and suggested I look into it. That's how I got my start in sport psychology.

I got on the waiting list for Springfield College's Athletic Counseling program. Being emotionally immature, I considered that door closed and thought that aspiration was over. A close friend I grew up with, Vicki Elkins, filled out the form to keep me on the wait list and told me to never close a door. Because of her, I ended up going to the Athletic Counseling program, where I connected with professors Al Petitpas, Judy Van Raalte, and Brit Brewer. They taught me about elite performance and how to help athletes through strong counseling skills, building relationships, and mental strategies.

Here I experienced significant growth because I started applying to myself what I was teaching athletes. To this day, my commitment to you and all my clients is that I won't advise someone or teach something that I don't genuinely believe works.

I am grateful for this program because it sparked a fire in me to help people help themselves. That's when I knew I wanted to become someone who could turn around dysfunctional leadership. I wanted to help good people find a way not to be manipulated, dominated, and stressed out by dominant personalities in positions of power. I also wanted to help dominant people realize they will get much more out of people if they focus less on manipulating and controlling others and more on engaging them.

So much time and energy are wasted when we worry and fall prey to our insecurities, but even worse, if we let dysfunctional people dominate us and set us in a direction we don't want to go, we are unable to reach our potential and can even do damage to ourselves. Dysfunctional dominance not only impacts our work life; it impacts our home life and our health.

Working with strong personalities others believed could never change was both challenging and inspiring. One turnaround I witnessed was with a sales executive named Trent. He always needed to win regardless of the costs and did not play well with others. The only thing he valued was meeting his sales goals. As a result, his team had to spend a great deal of energy and time dealing with what they called "the churn," his habit of changing meetings, deadlines, and presentations just to support whatever he needed in the moment.

Over time, these behaviors created resentment and his team began to underperform. Unfortunately, it took a decrease in sales for Trent to finally pay attention to how he was treating others and the negative impact it was having. Through a lot of conversation and some gentle yet strong nudges, Trent agreed to go down a path of getting results through effective leadership and influence rather than coercion and command. It was not easy, but Trent was able to restore his credibility and turn around his team's performance.

Dysfunction Creates Disruption

Every day millions of people suffer from workplace bullying. According to the Workplace Bullying Institute's U.S. Workplace Bullying Survey of Adult Americans, 30 percent of survey participants experienced bullying at work, 19 percent witnessed it, and 4 percent admitted to perpetrating it. That means 49 percent of US workers are affected by workplace bullying. If you apply those statistics to the country as a whole, that equates to 79.3 million people.[1]

Workplace bullying has been linked to the following:

- Stress-related illnesses, such as heart disease, high blood pressure, headaches, neck pain, ulcers, and decreased resistance to physical illness[2]
- Anxiety disorders, including generalized anxiety disorder, panic attacks, PTSD, and social anxiety disorder[3]
- Increased mental health prescriptions both for those who experience and those who witness bullying[4]
- Increased mental health costs[5]
- Trouble sleeping[6]

Many companies turn a blind eye to bullies because they get things done. Any negative effects are just the cost of doing business, right? But the truth is bullying costs businesses big bucks.

As just one example, according to the Workplace Bullying Institute survey, approximately 67 percent of those who experience workplace bullying either quit or are fired.[7] That staggering amount of turnover alone costs businesses billions of dollars a year.[8]

But turnover isn't the only cost to businesses. Workplace bullying also costs employers in terms of[9]

- lost productivity and innovation, as workers spend more time dealing with bullying behavior than actually working;
- absenteeism;
- increased HR and workers' compensation claims;
- increased employer healthcare costs; and
- negative PR, resulting in lost market share, opportunities, customers, talent, and reputation.

With nearly half of the US workforce affected by bullying behavior, the good news is that many want to become part of the solution.

Here's what I often hear from my clients:

- I want to learn a new way to be positively influential and make an impact.
- I want to stop being pushed around and manipulated.
- I don't want to keep wasting time at home talking about how someone treated me at work.
- I don't want to just give in or avoid people when they are dominant.
- I want to stop getting triggered by strong personalities.
- I want to be better at motivating myself and the people around me.
- I want to win without making someone else lose.
- I want more people to lead with values and purpose.
- I want to be more influential.
- I want to be part of initiatives that do good.

So, what's the solution?

We often believe the biggest obstacle to our success (whether psychological, physical, or financial) is other people. When faced with a dominant personality (or *alphas*, as we will refer to them in this book), we feel pressured to either fight back or cave in, both of which reinforce the cycle and give the alpha more power. Then we give them even *more* power by taking it personally and allowing our feelings to drive our behavior rather than what we want for the long term.

Of course, these typical reactions of taking the alpha head-on or caving to their every demand don't work.

The solution isn't to change the alpha. The solution is to change ourselves. We can choose to take ownership of our own power and learn to use it for good.

In other words, the solution is to become *BullyProof.*

What does it mean to be BullyProof? It's a mindset and skillset that equips you to accomplish the following:

1. Take the power out of the word *bully*.
2. Let go of the victim mentality.
3. Take ownership of your own power and develop *Value-Based Power*.
4. Master the approach of *Subtle Strength* to use your power for good.
5. Protect and build up others, your organization, and society.

Leveraging What We Have Learned Together

The Unabomber was a math prodigy turned mass killer. As part of a study at Harvard, he was psychologically tortured, which led to his disdain for the academic elite. In the Sparks School shooting, people recall the shooter saying, "You guys ruined my life, so I'm going to ruin yours."

The pattern is clear: if you're bullied and you don't know how to recover, you, in turn, become someone who has a higher potential to bully others.

These are two extreme examples. Let's take one that is more common. In my work I often partner with elite doctors. Many who have been trained at the most prestigious medical organizations have a certain mindset ingrained in them. It goes something like this: "No matter what, do not show a chink in the armor," or "You need to have the answer to every question." One elite person described it to me as being trained to go into meetings with a sword and a shield and to be sure to use the sword first.

How do you think you would interact with people if that was your mindset?

I've seen good people go wrong because of the intense insecurity these high-performing cultures breed. That is why in this book we won't just learn how the powerless can protect themselves and gain power but also how the powerful can learn to be less abusive and more inclusive. This shift benefits us all for the long term.

What's the Difference between Alphas and Bullies?

An *alpha* is someone who takes the lead in a situation regardless of whether they are the identified leader or subject-matter expert. Being an alpha is neither good nor bad. In contrast, I would define a *bully* as someone who consistently attempts to get what they want regardless of the costs. We'll talk much more about alphas and bullies throughout the book.

Over the last twenty-plus years, I have worked with underdogs and top dogs to help people become BullyProof. It's more important today than ever.

Who can benefit from becoming BullyProof?

- **People perceived as bullies.** In my experience working with alpha personalities, few of them realize their impact on others. They believe they're just getting things done and helping people! Everyone needs to take ownership of their impact on others and make sure they're not hurting more than they're helping.
- **People supervised by alpha personalities.** Often people who feel bullied by their boss have more power than they

think. The key is to recognize it and leverage it in a way that has the highest likelihood of producing a positive outcome.

- **Sales professionals.** Salespeople always need an edge when it comes to uncovering needs and influencing people. Too often salespeople come across as pushy and working their own agendas—or back down too quickly with tough potential clients. The key is to use Subtle Strength to *read before you lead* and gain credibility. If you can get in the door with a challenging and strong personality, mutual respect and loyalty kicks in, which leads to reoccurring sales opportunities.

- **Organizations that want to advocate for women and close the gap on gender bias.** Closing the gender gap is no longer a choice but a responsibility. Why does the solution lie on the shoulders of women when men created the situation? Closing the gap for good requires a partnership between people who are skilled at influencing female and male alphas—who are, in short, BullyProof.

- **People who work in dysfunctional environments.** Human resource departments try to help, but they often don't have the time, strategies, or expertise to coach people on how not to get caught up in dysfunction. By realizing your options and your strength style, you can learn how to buffer yourself from dysfunction and protect others. Whether you work for a Fortune 500 company or a two-person business, Subtle Strength can help you not only transform yourself but your entire organization.

- **Surgeon leaders.** Not to pick on surgeons, but statistics show workplace bullying is particularly strong in the healthcare industry. I also know from experience that most surgeons believe vulnerability is a weakness. However, vulnerability is exactly what your team members need to see from you. If you want to do more than simply cut people (inside or outside the operating room), Subtle Strength will help you keep your edge and grow your leadership influence.

- **Wealth managers.** People who work in the finance industry often need to partner with and influence successful, driven clients. The strategies in this book will help you better understand what makes performance-oriented people tick and how to diversify your approach to build credibility and influence capital.

- **Service providers.** The service industry, whether it is hospitality, dining, or flight support for private flyers, is full of unique personalities who have a lot of power. The BullyProof approach teaches you how not to get triggered and how to demonstrate calm confidence so you can maintain key relationships while respectfully influencing people in your desired direction. The shift from taking things personally to focusing on leveraging Value-Based Power is a game changer.

Becoming BullyProof

What if you could become BullyProof? Even better, what if you could level the playing field and become the Robin Hood of power in your organization? Becoming BullyProof is not about stealing power from those who have it and giving it to those who don't. It's about helping those who feel powerless take ownership of the power they *already have* and preventing people in powerful positions from using abusive power.

Core to the process of becoming BullyProof is developing *ego agility*. My mentor in the field of performance psychology, Al Petitpas, taught me the importance of having "just the right amount of ego." What he meant by this is to believe in yourself enough that you understand the value of collaborating and bringing in other experts.

On one hand, ego agility is the ability to temporarily release your agenda and your raw inner drive to win or be right in the moment. It does not mean that you can't win. It just means you need to be involved in a different game, one in which you are secure and confident enough to give up some control in the short term to gain influence capital in the long term.

Ego agility also means taking ownership of your power, having confidence in yourself, and acting on your ambitions—without getting your ego overly involved. You will find the more ego agility you demonstrate, the more credibility and influence capital you will have. Ego agility will also ensure that when you do become BullyProof, you will use your powers for good, to build up yourself, other people, your organization, and society as a whole.

Whether you're in a position of power and want to leverage it more effectively, are lacking power and want to become more influential, or want an edge in working with strong personalities, here is your roadmap to becoming BullyProof for yourself, others, your organization, and society at-large.

Part 1 begins with you. First, you'll take back ownership of your own power by redefining both power and strength. You'll learn about a new approach to power called *Value-Based Power* (VBP), the key framework for becoming BullyProof. VBP is balanced and intentional influence across four core areas: self, others, organization, and society. Instead of getting pulled into and stuck in the polarity of dominance versus submission, to leverage your

VBP you'll learn about the value of *Subtle Strength*, which demonstrates calm confidence, backbone, and respect. It helps the powerless gain power, the powerful be more mindful of their impact, and everyone win more together.

Becoming BullyProof requires mastering both.

In the remainder of Part 1, you'll learn how to use Value-Based Power and Subtle Strength to positively influence yourself and others. We'll cover all things alpha, the neuroscience of stress and influence so you can more effectively lead yourself, and practical strategies to positively influence alphas in a variety of situations.

For example, I will introduce you to a framework for engaging and influencing people called Motivational Currency®. This approach is based on decades of research by Harvard psychologist David McClelland. He looked at social motives and what drives our behavior internally. The core four motivators of Motivational Currency are *Performance, People, Power*, and *Purpose*. We will take a deep dive into this approach, and by the end of the book, you will be able to assess these motivators and others so you can collaborate and influence in an intentional manner.

Then, in Part 2, you'll expand your BullyProof skills to positively influence your organization and society at large. You will be equipped to lead with Subtle Strength in times of crisis, learn why alpha women are your best allies in creating a BullyProof culture, put people above politics to strengthen your organization and society, and create your own plan for becoming BullyProof and helping others do the same.

If you've picked up this book, I'm guessing you've reached a pain point where you are motivated to make a change, or maybe you have an internal drive to achieve more or be the best at something. You may even know a lot about power dynamics and bullies, but for some reason, you haven't been able to put it into practice. Either way, you are no longer willing to accept the status quo. You don't want to run from this problem any longer—you want to rise to the occasion, grow through the challenge, and do whatever it takes to positively influence your situation.

That's exactly what this book will help you do. Of course, it's not enough just to *know* what to do; you must be motivated and equipped to actually *do* it, especially when stakes are high. For that reason, every chapter will give you an opportunity to apply what you've learned and share it with others.

However, this is not a step-by-step playbook; it is a principle-based guide to help you mitigate risks and increase probability of success. There is never a one-size-fits-all solution. Every situation calls for different approaches and every rule has exceptions. Although you'll typically want to lead with Subtle Strength, sometimes you'll need to use a dominant or a submissive strength style for a purpose. The principles and strategies you learn will help you know which type of strength style to use, and when.

Ready to Grow?

No one should go through life or work feeling powerless. You can take ownership of your power and use it for good—not just for yourself, but for your family, your coworkers, your organization, and your community too.

Becoming BullyProof is not just about me and you, it's about creating environments where people feel powerful and are willing to play a role in one another's success. Together we can make significant progress in turning around dysfunctional behavior and decreasing the time and emotional energy we waste on people who aren't thinking about us.

xxvi | **BULLY*PROOF***

To support your BullyProof journey, I encourage you to visit OnPointAdvising.com/BullyProof to download free exclusive resources.

One of my favorite quotes by Frank Zappa has served me well as I take on new adventures: "A mind is like a parachute. It doesn't work if it's not open." I invite you to remind yourself to keep an open mind, and you will see how much our minds matter when it comes to influence and your success.

Let's start becoming BullyProof.

Part 1

BullyProof Yourself and Others

CHAPTER 1

Value-Based Power: A Balanced Approach to Influence

A certain executive in a tech company was known for driving results. The board of directors and the rest of the C-suite viewed him as an excellent leader because his teams consistently brought innovative products to market and hit their metrics every quarter. The problem was that he achieved these results by micromanaging his team, and the team was slowly and silently burning out. His timelines became unrealistic as he expected his employees to be working at their peak every moment of every day. When team members couldn't deliver according to his expectations, he typically grew impatient and often yelled out of frustration.

The result was a working climate of fear, which created resentment. Employees were responding to this type of dominance by becoming passive and trying to avoid the executive. This created a cycle where the executive would think less and less of the team and mistake their disengagement as lack of competence.

One of the executive's most talented team members was now dreading going to work. She felt she had lost her creativity and motivation and was even wondering if she was getting depressed. She certainly wasn't going to talk to her boss about it because she feared losing her job, but she finally found the courage to talk to a coworker.

She was surprised to discover the rest of her team was feeling the same way. Among the team, self-doubt shifted to anger and blame. The colleagues realized they had no space to create the level of results their boss was demanding, and they decided the problem was their boss's dysfunctional leadership. He just didn't understand what it took to be creatively productive. One by one, they left the company for what they believed would be a more supportive work environment.

Meanwhile, the executive had no idea how the team members felt because he assumed everyone was like him: driven, achievement oriented, and focused on getting things done regardless of the cost. In their exit interviews, he received no feedback about his management style except for vague statements about how they had learned a lot at this organization but were ready to move on. He attributed the turnover to the fact that nobody stayed in one job for long anymore. Obviously, they couldn't take the pressure of working at a top-tier organization, and he would just need to find others who could.

The Cost of Dysfunctional Power

Whom did you relate with more: the executive or the team members? Or both?

As we saw in the introduction, the cost of dysfunctional power is staggering. Not only does it cost employees in terms of health, self-esteem, productivity, and steady employment, it costs the dysfunctionally dominant supervisor in terms of stress, turnover, and talent lost. Often times it ends up diminishing the executive's credibility and derailing the executive's career.

As we talk about the cost of dysfunctional power, I want to acknowledge the pioneering work of others. One of the greatest thought leaders in the field of organizational psychology is Adam Grant of Wharton. He doesn't know it, but his work always influences my thinking, rethinking, and advising. I sent him an email out of the blue asking him about any work he knew of related to bullying in the workplace. He was gracious enough to respond and told me about the work of Bob Sutton, who has done incredible work on abusive power and its impact on people and business. Sutton's book *The No A$$hole Rule: Building a Civilized Workplace and Surviving One That Isn't* helped me better understand the true costs of dysfunction and abusive power, and he is truly a pioneer in this space.[10]

I can't put this strongly enough: If you're keeping someone around who's a high performer but dysfunctionally dominant, you may think you're driving performance, but you're actually hurting productivity. Any positive results you can see are decimated by the damage you can't see.

On the other hand, if you're experiencing dysfunctional dominance at your workplace, there's a tremendous cost to doing nothing as well.

I want you to know you have another choice: You can choose to own your power. You can choose to be a leader in these dysfunctional situations and influence them in a positive way.

Own Your Power

Regardless of our personality, at some point all of us will fall into a victim mentality. It happens to everyone, and it's normal. The keys are to (1) recognize when we have fallen into a victim mentality and (2) know how to shift to an *ownership* mentality so we don't make tough situations worse. I also want you to be able to identify this process in others so you can help them help themselves, creating a positive cycle of confidence and initiative.

When we are in a victim mentality, our feelings become facts and we forget we have the ability to positively influence any situation. Believing that you don't have any control can be very dangerous, as can only focusing on what you can't control. When you focus on what is happening to you rather than what you can make happen, you miss out on opportunities and train your mind to give up rather than have hope.

In every situation you have a choice: Am I going to be a victim, or am I going to be an owner?

Our minds are very powerful, and we can either help ourselves by guiding our thoughts or hurt ourselves by letting them go on autopilot. Here is a roadmap that outlines two pathways: the victim cycle, where things happen to you, and the ownership cycle, where you make things happen.

Both cycles start at the same place, with an event, and they end up in very different places with different outcomes.[11]

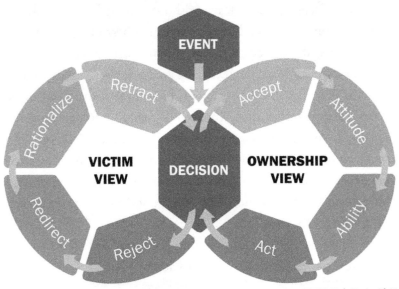

©2015 Rob Fazio, PhD
OnPoint Advising, Inc.

Figure 1.1. The Pathway to Ownership

First, an event occurs. With every event, we have a decision to make: Will we reject what has happened and resist it, or will we accept what has happened and do what we can to improve the situation?

This decision, reject or accept, sets the cycle of victim or ownership in motion.

If you choose to reject the event and resist what is happening, the victim cycle begins, where we focus on what others aren't doing rather than what we can be doing to adapt or get ahead. We *redirect and blame*, talking about what is wrong rather than what can go right. We *rationalize*, explaining to ourselves and others why our victim mentality is the best response to the situation. We may even end up creating a victim alliance, where others join our pity party and enter into the victim cycle with us. Finally, we *retract*, where we disengage and "leave without leaving." Eventually we may leave physically too, like the team members in our example.

However, if you accept the event instead of rejecting it, you enter the ownership cycle. Accepting an event doesn't mean agreeing with it; it just means you're ready to deal with it and move towards action rather than reaction. When you accept what has happened, your *attitude* becomes more positive, which provides more fuel for action. It also increases your *ability* to move forward and develop new skills to adjust and adapt. And this increased ability results in more action, where you continue to *act* intentionally and focus forward.

Even if you fall into the victim cycle, you don't have to stay there. You can decide at any time to accept your situation, rather than reject it, and enter the ownership cycle.

Over time you can train yourself to accept situations more quickly and, therefore, take ownership of your power more often and become more action oriented even in times of crisis. We'll talk more about how to train your brain to take ownership throughout the book.

What are the benefits of choosing to own your power? What positive results do you want to create for yourself, for others, for your organization, for society?

What is the cost of choosing not to own your power?

Once you become skilled at taking ownership of your power and influence, it's time to take responsibility for your impact.

To do that, I invite you to consider a new vision of power: Value-Based Power.

Value-Based Power

I attended an event where a speaker was talking about power. The speaker asked the question, "How do you feel when you don't have power?" The audience responded with a host of responses, such as defeated, demotivated, beaten, angry, lost, disenfranchised. I raised my hand and responded, "Motivated!"

"When you are powerless?" the speaker asked with a puzzled look of disapproval.

I responded, "Yes, if I don't have power, I am motivated to get it and share it." With a little laughter, I added, "Perhaps it has something to do with being Sicilian."

Power is an important part of business and life. When we don't have power, we often lack motivation. When we do have power, we have the opportunity to do a lot of good, and we also run the risk of doing potential harm.

Positional authority also magnifies the impact of someone's power. The power that comes with someone's position can be used to elevate people or beat them down.

When we experience dysfunctional power situations over and over, it's easy to believe power is bad. But power isn't inherently bad. It's just often misused.

The type of power you exhibit is directly related to your intentions and motivations. *Value-Based Power* (VBP) is an approach toward power where you intentionally use your influence to act according to your values, balanced across four areas: self, others, organization, and society. Our values guide us and give us strength and courage to act, even in challenging situations.

Figure 1.2. Value-Based Power

This book isn't just about influencing alphas; it's about fully owning your power so you can use it for good. In fact, connecting your values and your influence can give you courage you may not otherwise have access to. For example, if you are hesitant to raise an unpopular view to a dominant person but then shift your focus to how your view will help others, you will be more likely to speak up.

One common mistake leaders make is focusing on only one or two of these four areas. Everyone has a default focus under pressure, and there's nothing wrong with that. It's also okay to be ambitious and self-focused. But the way to increase influence and engage even the most dominant people is to balance your focus across all four areas.

Let's take a look at four leaders with varying levels of VBP.

Leader A oversaw portfolio managers in an asset manager firm. He focused solely on his own ambitions and success, so much so that his team decided they were no longer going to put on good trades because they wanted their boss to fail.

Leader B was a professor who was passionate about advising and helping his students. He had a very strong focus on helping others and helping out the college in any way he could. While his intentions were noble and he was a true giver, he did not spend time on his own ambitions and elevating himself. He often got pushed around by strong personalities because he did not have a track record of personal successes.

Leader C was a nonprofit leader who only focused on public service and youth development. He never advocated for himself or other people on his team. Over time he became cynical and his followership decreased because he wasn't able to get the resources needed to be successful. Eventually he burnt out.

Leaders with balanced VBP take action to focus on self, others, the organization, and society. One example is Grace Kaznecki, an aware adaptive alpha (we'll talk more about what this means in the next chapter) who is the wealth management chief administrative officer at Wells Fargo. She is known as someone who gets things done and brings others along. She is ambitious and delivers. Grace has a passion for building high-performing teams who are focused on collaboration and developing one another. She also is laser focused on the business and organization, always challenging the status quo and looking to make the organization better.

Inside and outside of work, Grace is very purpose driven. She is on the board of the nonprofit Hold the Door for Others, which was inspired by September 11 and focuses on challenging and equipping people to grow through loss and adversity. She is also involved in many initiatives that focus on doing good for society. The result of Grace's approach is that she is able to get more for her people, herself, her business, and society. One of her guiding metaphors is to be the Tinkerbell of leadership and sprinkle positivity and performance to those she connects with. You know when someone leads with VBP because the more power they gain, the more they share it with others to do good.

> Where do you focus your power?
>
> Who do you see exhibiting strong, balanced Value-Based Power?

How do you know if you're focusing well enough on each of the four areas? You can use the concept of VBP as a checklist. For example, if you are making a difficult decision, you can ask yourself whether you are *aware* of the values, ambitions, and challenges of yourself, other stakeholders, the organization as a whole, and society, and if you are taking action in each of those areas.

You can also use it as an evaluation tool for past events. If you've just finished a challenging meeting, you can ask yourself whether you were aware of your own values, ambitions, and challenges, as well as those of others in the meeting, the organization, and society as a whole, and if you were taking action in each of those areas accordingly.

The key question to ask is, "What is my intention and motivation in this situation, and how can I make sure it is balanced across all four areas?"

		Was I aware?	Did I take action?
Self	Values		
	Ambitions		
	Challenges		
Others	Values		
	Ambitions		
	Challenges		
Organization	Values		
	Ambitions		
	Challenges		
Society	Values		
	Ambitions		
	Challenges		

Figure 1.3. Value-Based Power Worksheet

If you'd like to download an editable version of this Value-Based Power worksheet that functions as both a checklist and an evaluation tool, go to OnPointAdvising.com/BullyProof.

Strength Styles

Even if you have taken ownership of your power and your impact in all four areas of VBP, the ways you attempt to influence a dysfunctionally dominant person can yield different results.

When it comes to influencing alphas, we actually have a continuum of strength styles available to us: *submissive, subtle, overt,* and *dominant.*

Strength Styles

Features	Strength Style			
	Submissive	**Subtle**	**Overt**	**Dominant**
Calm Confidence	High	High	Medium	Low
Respect	Medium	High	High	Low
Backbone	Low	High	High	High
Feelings First	High	High	Medium	Low
Force First	Low	Medium	Medium	High
Temperament	Reactive	Strategic	Strategic	Reactive
Identity	Victim	Leader	Leader	Dominator
Short-Term Impact	Lose/Win	Win/Win	Win/Lose	Win/Lose
Long-Term Impact	Lose/Lose	Win/Win	Win/Win	Lose/Lose or Lose/Win
VBP Focus	Self	All	All	Self

Figure 1.4. Strength Styles

The *submissive* strength style means being passive. While in the short term it may provide relief from dealing with an alpha, this approach also unintentionally gives a bully permission to keep dominating. If used unintentionally, it typically focuses on the needs of the self.

The *Subtle Strength* style is intentional influence that demonstrates backbone and respect through calm confidence. This approach gives you the best chance of not emotionally triggering someone who is dysfunctionally dominant and escalating a situation. It also allows you to engage people and be a positive influence because you are focused on all four areas of VBP: self, others, organization, and society.

The *overt* strength style is assertive, clear, but not aggressive. It also allows you to focus on all four facets of VBP.

The *dominant* strength style, in comparison, is direct, coercive, and has no regard for impact on others. If used unintentionally, like the submissive style, it focuses solely on self.

As part of our research on strength styles, we asked the following question: "When are you most likely to allow the other person to use the armrest on a plane?"

- Seventy-one percent said they were willing to share or give up the armrest when the other person either leaves it open or asks if he or she can use it.
- Only 17 percent were willing to share when the other person took over the armrest first.

This is an excellent example of why dominant power does not work. Less than 20 percent of people are willing to yield to you if you use force or pressure. On the other hand, over 70 percent of people are willing to share resources, compromise, or yield to you if you invite them to be part of the decision.

What do these strength styles look like in practice? Let's say a dominant alpha tells you, "You waste too much time asking the sales team their opinions. They are adults; they need to hit their numbers or we will find someone else who will."

The table below provides an overview of how each strength style might respond and its corresponding impact.

Strength Style	Sample Response	Likely Impact
Submissive	"I'm sorry. I will be sure to focus on what you think is most important."	The alpha believes they had a successful leadership moment and will use the same approach next time.
Subtle	"Thank you for the reminder. I agree the numbers are critical to success. Your clarity is helpful. Do you think it's possible some people perform better when they are able to contribute to our sales approach?"	The alpha feels validated and thinks their subordinate is aligned with them. This response makes them open to building upon their black-and-white approach.
Overt	"While the numbers are important, I have to tell you we will get better numbers over time if we engage our sales team."	While the alpha appreciates direct dialogue, this approach challenges their authority, and they will either come back with more dominance or match the overt strength.

Dominant	"You don't know what you're talking about. You're removed from the day-to-day. The team needs to feel they are part of the process. Go ahead and see what happens if you send that message."	The alpha will fear they are losing control and will double down on dominance to reestablish authority.

As you can see, successful influence typically comes from *Subtle Strength* and *overt strength*. Both styles are based in emotional agility, intentionality, and strategy.

Key Definitions

- **Alpha**: Someone who takes the lead in a situation regardless of whether they are the identified leader or subject-matter expert

- **Bully**: Someone who consistently attempts to get what they want regardless of the costs

- **BullyProof**: Taking ownership of your own power and protecting yourself and others from dysfunctional behavior

- **Subtle Strength**: Intentional influence that uses calm confidence to demonstrate backbone, and respect

- **Value-Based Power**: Balanced influence in four core areas of focus: self, others, organization, and society

What's Your Strength Style?

Everyone has their own default strength style. The goal is not to change your default style but to be aware of it and to shift to another strength style when you choose. Also, although the Subtle Strength and overt strength styles are the most effective in influencing alphas, there may be times when you will want to use a dominant style, such as in a crisis situation, or a submissive style, such as when a bully is **triggered** and the best strategy is to end the current interaction as quickly as possible and address it later. Being aware of your default strength style will allow you to be intentional about what shifts to make. It will also help us limit the risk of only using a strength style that is most comfortable to us but does not help us accomplish what we want.

Below is a quiz to help you learn your strength style. Please rate the extent to which each of the statements describes you.

Directions: For each item, score yourself on a scale from 1 (strongly disagree) to 6 (strongly agree). Add up the total score for each category. The highest score is your default strength style.

Submissive	
	If someone pushes their point of view, I don't give mine.
	I don't set the direction in a conversation.
	I rarely get what I want.
	People describe me as passive.
	I avoid conflict.
	I don't advocate for myself if it causes conflict.

Subtle	
	I am intentional about how I influence people.
	I am able to gently get others to see my point of view.
	I use compliments when influencing someone.
	I agree with people so they are more likely to agree with me.
	I use humor when I influence people.
	I have calm confidence when I disagree with people.

Overt	
	I am assertive.
	I advocate for myself.
	I am comfortable disagreeing with other points of view.
	I take debates head on.
	I focus on getting my point across in conversations.
	I communicate directly with clarity.

Dominant	
	I am good at getting what I want.
	I direct most conversations.
	I can control a conversation.
	I often change people's minds.
	I make most decisions in my interactions.
	I usually win negotiations.

Your Strength Style Profile

Add up your totals for each of the strength styles. There likely will be one highest and one lowest score.

Submissive	Subtle	Overt	Dominant

What is your default strength style?

Which strength style would you like to become more proficient in?

If your default strength was submissive, overt, or dominant, how can you increase your score in Subtle Strength so that your Subtle Strength is available when needed?

If you discovered your default style is submissive, don't despair. Adapting and leveraging different strength styles is a skill just like any other. It takes motivation to grow, leaning into discomfort, and belief in yourself. At first your mind may play tricks on you and convince you that you aren't able to shift from submissive to Subtle Strength or overt strength, but I've seen it happen many times. The first step is to realize that it is possible, and the way to do that is to find people who have evolved and shifted from a default submissive style to building their strength and using different styles.

It often begins with a minor shift that creates some positive momentum. Don't underestimate the power of positive experiences. For the golfers out there, it's similar to playing a bad round but then remembering that one shot where you felt true compression and sent the ball where you wanted. Focusing on that small win and that feeling of things going the way we want helps us realize we have it in us and increases our motivation to keep working at it.

BullyProof Strategy #1: Own Your Power

1. If you find yourself caught in a victim mentality, choose to enter the ownership cycle by accepting the situation rather than rejecting or resisting it.
2. Use the Value-Based Power framework as a checklist for your next decision or to evaluate a recent interaction. How balanced is your influence?
3. Take the Strength Styles quiz and identify your default strength style.

By choosing to own our power, taking responsibility for our power through the framework of Value-Based Power, and understanding the strength styles available to us, we have set the foundation for becoming BullyProof. If we want to use our Value-Based Power to positively influence alphas, we need to know more about who we're dealing with. So, let's take a look at all things alpha.

Awareness, Application, and Alliances

What insights did I have in this chapter?

What will I apply and when?

With whom will I share what I learned?

CHAPTER 2:

All Things Alpha

A resident surgeon at a well-known institution shared a story with me. She was at the top of her class, a competent and kind person who believed in helping people. She worked for an insecure, dominant surgeon who was chair of the department. The chair of surgery was internationally known, well published, and self-absorbed. She was also a flat-out bully. When communicating with her teams, she had one approach: I'm right, and you need to listen and learn from me.

She regularly talked over people and used the Socratic method as a weapon, leaving her surgical team feeling inadequate and incompetent. She was as sharp and proficient at cutting people with words as she was with a scalpel. She was such a bully that during surgeries her team would not tell her information—including patient information crucial for a successful surgery—for fear of her lashing out at them or negatively impacting their career. Members of the operating staff were known to try to have other surgeons take over during surgeries. Despite being perceived as a good surgeon, because people feared her and regularly withheld information, she actually wasn't.

The story ends with the resident surgeon not only leaving the organization but going to a different country to finish her medical training out of fear of retribution.

Contrast that leader with a seasoned executive in banking. I have had the privilege firsthand of seeing Joy Zaben lead people through an acquisition, lead an organization through the pandemic by taking on the paycheck protection program, and build cultures of trust and performance. There is a lot that is special about Joy, but what truly makes her stand out? She cares about relationships and results and is willing to take the lead in the most difficult situations.

Joy is the type of person that when you meet her you can feel her love of people and desire to elevate others. She oozes credibility and positivity. At the same time, her approach to leadership and partnering allows her to give tough messages to people in power. She has the rare balance of someone who naturally influences through Value-Based Power and Subtle Strength. There is never a question of where her motivation lies. She recently became the chief of staff to the chief of strategy at Visa, and I can imagine she is building trust throughout the organization and being a positive force for the business.

Which leader is an alpha: the chair of surgery or the banking executive?

Answer: Both. The difference is that one is also a bully.

What Is an Alpha?

Let's begin with defining some key terms.

When I use the term *alpha*, I'm referring to someone who takes charge of situations whether or not they are the identified leader or subject-matter expert. We are not talking about alphas in the biological or evolutionary sense; we're simply talking about patterns of behaviors.

Alphas are critical to the success of almost any endeavor. They are the people who thrive when they drive. They naturally take control of situations and make decisions quickly.

A *bully*, on the other hand, is someone who consistently attempts to get what they want regardless of the cost.

Oftentimes people who are perceived to be bullies are alphas who are just doing what they do, which is take charge. All bullies are alphas, but not all alphas are bullies. As we saw in the two examples of alphas at the beginning of the chapter, there's a big difference between taking charge of a situation and insisting on getting what you want.

If we blame alphas alone for dysfunctional power situations, we're missing a big piece of the puzzle. Trust me, I am not excusing bullying behavior, but I am suggesting that we look at the big picture and take a different approach.

Rather than get pulled into the typical reactions to alpha behavior, you can learn to align with their ambitions so you can be a positive influence rather than a victim. That's what I mean by *BullyProof*.

The problem is we are programmed to hate bullies because of the way they make us feel. When we feel stressed or triggered by bullying behavior, we are automatically pulled into a polarizing limited mindset. We also all have something called *confirmation bias*, where our minds will actively find ways to reinforce any story we believe. For example, if you believe one political party has the correct view over the other, you will find ways to reinforce that belief. The danger of confirmation bias is people walk around on a daily basis not realizing how much of their thinking is automatic and narrow-minded. Becoming aware of how you are limiting yourself is critical to your success and your influence capital. We'll talk more about how stress affects our brain and our biases in chapter 3, and the impact of those biases in chapter 10.

Why are we empathetic toward people with depression, anxiety, or schizophrenia, but not bullies? While I'm not condoning what bullies do, I do think, in order to break the cycle, we need to understand how they think and develop some empathy for them so as to influence them for good.

So if all bullies are alphas but not all alphas are bullies, how can you tell if someone is an alpha? Here's a quiz you can take to find out.

Think of someone you know who might be an alpha.

Does this person do any of the following?

- take charge of most situations
- overtly disagree with people
- have a strong point of view
- thrive in competitive situations
- break the rules when needed
- communicate with authority
- get stressed if they are not making the important decisions
- have a preference for taking action
- redirect conversations
- tell more than ask
- give their point of view whether asked or not

If this person does more than three of these things, you are likely dealing with an alpha.

Now that you've identified whether the person you were thinking of is an alpha, go back and take the quiz for yourself.

Are you an alpha?

Our Findings about Alphas

Our research showed the following findings:

- Less than 25 percent of people perceive themselves as being alphas.
- Self-identified alphas
  - » are happier;
  - » are more engaged at work;
  - » are more confident;
  - » feel like they can make an impact;
  - » are more willing to do hard things like have tough conversations; and
  - » are more willing to work towards their goals compared to the 77 percent of people who do not perceive themselves as alphas.
- Sixty percent of non-alphas view themselves as successful versus 95 percent of alphas.
- Men and women do not report differently when it comes to alphas.
- Sixty-six percent of alphas reported that they manage people versus 40 percent of non-alphas.

The Four Types of Alphas

Once you have identified whether someone is an alpha (including yourself), you can consider what type of alpha they are. The more you understand someone, the better equipped you are to adapt to connect with them and speak their language. There are four types of alphas, and the four types are a function of two factors: *awareness* and *adaptiveness*.

Awareness means the person has an understanding of their behavior and the impact it has on other people.

Adaptiveness means the person is capable of varying their communication style to create the best possible outcomes.

In chapter 1, we discussed the four strength styles: submissive, subtle, overt, and dominant. Remember, although the overt strength and Subtle Strength styles are more likely to positively influence alphas, good judgment is critical. If you're golfing and you end up in the bunker, you don't use your driver. Similarly, you might choose to use a dominant style if you're in a crisis situation, or perhaps you choose a submissive style as part of an overall influence strategy if you know an alpha is easily triggered by the topic at hand. In short, you need the right tools for the job.

Also, the type of alpha you are isn't a function of character. You can be any one of these four types and still be a good person, and you can be any one of these types and still get good results. What really matters is whether you are using Value-Based Power—intentionally considering your values as they relate to self, others, organization, and society. This means that even if you're an unaware nonadaptive alpha using a dominant style, if you're also using Value-Based Power, people probably won't see you as a bully.

Aware Nonadaptive

Aware nonadaptive alphas are aware they want to be in charge and understand their impact on people and situations. They are helpful in situations where they are aligned with your interests. The challenge is that they tend to choose not to adjust their communication style with various situations and people. As a result, they can often be perceived as stubborn or reactive.

I was advising a doctor who knew he was perceived as an alpha and knew the impact he had on his team, but he just wanted things to get done. His primary goal was to build his practice, and he viewed his staff as underperformers with victim mentalities. Rather than making some shifts to engage the staff and determine who was dedicated to the hospital system and who wasn't, he charged ahead with an even stronger and coercive approach. As a result, engagement and patient-satisfaction scores went down, and he lost key talent.

It is not enough to be aware; you also have to be willing to adapt. Aware nonadaptive alphas can at times demonstrate a lot of bullying behavior even though they know they are demonstrating dominant behavior and know the impact they are having on others and how that can jeopardize results.

As someone who has chosen to be BullyProof, how might you productively influence an aware nonadaptive alpha?

Aware Nonadaptive Alpha

"I know what it takes to win, and we're going to win. I also know that people think I'm a bully, but I don't care as long as we get good results."

Strength style to influence: overt or Subtle Strength

In general, if someone is an aware alpha, it's faster and more effective to use an overt strength style because they're aware of their tendencies and probably won't be blindsided by direct feedback. With unaware alphas, a Subtle Strength style is more effective because you are less likely to trigger them.

Here's what that could look like. If you wanted to influence the aware nonadaptive doctor mentioned above with an overt strength style, you might say, "I need to be up front with you. I think the approach you're taking is having a negative impact on what you actually want to accomplish. I know you want patient satisfaction to be strong, and I also know you want to build your practice. I can help you think through ways you can do that."

A Subtle Strength style might use a more indirect approach, while still sending the important message. If you knew the surgeon's primary goal was to grow his practice, you might say, "You've been doing this for a long time and know what works. Based on your expertise, how about we talk through what the success factors are in growing your practice?" After listening to their response, you might then ask, "I've seen other surgeons grow their business by treating their staff similar to the way they treat their patients and their families. Would that be a relevant approach?" Ask the surgeon questions without hurting his ego, but if he's still not getting it, you can shift toward a more overt style. For aware nonadaptive alphas, the goal is to demonstrate a partnership focused on helping them get what they want but without triggering them or others.

Who in your life is an aware nonadaptive alpha?

Are you an aware nonadaptive alpha?

Based on your responses, what change could you make in your next interaction to increase your influence?

Unaware Adaptive

Unaware adaptive alphas don't realize they are alphas and don't realize their impact on others. They tend to be focused on themselves and their personal goals, and they are typically seeking to influence others to get what they want for themselves. Although they don't realize they tend to dominate the situation, they do tend to be very aware of all the moving parts of their business or organization, so they're very responsive to change. That means they tend to be flexible and respond appropriately to different people and situations in order to achieve the outcomes they want. They are less threatening than the aware nonadaptive alpha and tend to get the benefit of the doubt when they make missteps. Their primary challenge is that they tend to get triggered and react rather than intentionally respond.

For example, if our surgeon leader was an unaware adaptive alpha with the goal of building his practice, he might treat his patients kindly but get very impatient with his staff.

Unaware Adaptive Alpha

"I'm focused on achieving my own goals, and I'll adapt as needed in order to meet them."

Strength style to influence: Subtle Strength or overt

If you're seeking to influence an unaware adaptive alpha, a Subtle Strength style is the most effective, but an overt style might also work, depending on the personality and situation.

For example, if you wanted to influence the unaware adaptive surgeon, you would lead with Subtle Strength by bringing his behavior into his awareness, starting with his positive behavior. "You're really good at showing the patient you care." Stockpile some compliments over time. Then, at the right time, ask a strategic question: "Did you notice in this situation how the resident didn't respond well?" The surgeon would likely adapt to this feedback because he would know that good team dynamics are also part of being a good surgeon, and the change would help him meet his goals.

If you had developed some relationship capital or even trust with this leader over time, you could start with the overt approach. "I noticed that the resident didn't respond well when you called them out in front of the group."

Who in your life is an unaware adaptive alpha?

Are you an unaware adaptive alpha?

Based on your responses, what change could you make in your next interaction to increase your influence?

Unaware Nonadaptive

Unaware nonadaptive alphas are the most challenging type of alpha to work with. These are the people most often thought of as bullies or even narcissists, which we'll cover later in this chapter. They tend to be solely focused on self and have particular difficulty demonstrating Value-Based Power. They believe in winning at all costs and do not care who they hurt in the process. Oftentimes they rise in an organization quickly because they can get results in the short term. However, they often eventually fail because they have strained so many relationships. If you are not aligned with their ambitions, they can be dangerous.

If our surgeon was an unaware nonadaptive alpha, he would look and act like an unaware *adaptive* alpha, but when something is brought to his attention, he wouldn't change or care.

Unaware Nonadaptive Alpha

"I'm focused on achieving my own goals, and I'll do whatever it takes to meet them, regardless of the cost."

Strength style to influence: Subtle Strength or overt

To influence an unaware nonadaptive alpha, the best approach is to use Subtle Strength over time, as with an aware nonadaptive alpha. If you have built a relationship of mutual respect with this person, an overt approach might also be effective.

But in some situations, your strength style alone won't be enough to positively influence the unaware nonadaptive alpha. You might need to build an alliance with an aware adaptive alpha or even leave the organization. Skip to chapter 10 if you want to see how to build alliances, but be sure to come back and finish All Things Alpha. There is nothing wrong with leaving a situation where you recognize you have little to no chance of changing it for the better. As an executive advisor who often sees situations like this, it bothers me a lot when people stay stuck in these situations, like my dad did when I was younger. The cost to self, health, and relationships just isn't worth it sometimes. Exhibiting Value-Based Power includes focusing on yourself too. In chapter 7, we'll talk more about how to tell if someone is exhibiting bullying behaviors and how to respond.

Who in your life is an unaware nonadaptive alpha?

Are you an unaware adaptive alpha?

Based on your responses, what change could you make in your next interaction to increase your influence?

Aware Adaptive

Aware adaptive alphas have strong self and social awareness and high emotional intelligence. They know they are alphas and they tend to take charge; they also appreciate the importance of letting others take the lead. They effectively influence themselves so they can influence others. Aware adaptive alphas often have high credibility, especially when they use their power for good.

What makes the biggest difference is what type of power they use and whether they are willing to play a role in the success of others and their organization. When this type of alpha uses Value-Based Power, everyone wins. Aware adaptive alphas who leverage Value-Based Power are the most important people to build alliances with. They can influence the other three alpha types because they command respect and are masters at using overt and Subtle Strength. Their challenge is that they may use bullying techniques when stressed or under pressure.

Let's say our surgeon leader mentioned above was an aware adaptive alpha with the same goal: to build his practice. Under pressure, he might also treat his team poorly when focused on achieving a particular outcome. The difference is that he will likely approach someone later and apologize. If that person brought it up first, he would likely recognize his behavior and want to change.

Aware Adaptive Alpha

"I know I tend to take charge, although I enjoy allowing others to take charge too. I want to influence myself so I can make a positive impact for myself, others, our organization, and our society."

Strength style to influence: overt or Subtle Strength

If you wanted to influence the situation, as with any alpha, you still must demonstrate a level of strength in how you show up. As with aware nonadaptive alphas, the most effective approach is overt strength, and Subtle Strength can also be effective if time is not a factor or if the aware adaptive alpha is easily triggered by the particular topic.

For example, with the aware adaptive surgeon, you could use an overt strength style as with the unaware adaptive alpha. But because this alpha is aware of his tendencies, you would only need to mention it briefly to be effective: "I noticed that resident didn't respond well when you called them out in front of the group."

Or if time is not a factor and/or you knew this was a delicate subject for this leader, you could use a Subtle Strength style: "We both know how important building your practice is to you and the department. In your interactions with patients, I've noticed your effective approach of seeking to understand your patients and provide them with the best possible guidance. This is helping you build a great reputation in the community. I've also noticed that our staff gets quiet and doesn't offer their point of view from time to time. This usually happens when they are redirected and harshly criticized in the front of the group. I wonder if treating our staff with the same level of care as you treat our patients could help us grow even more." If this subtle approach doesn't seem to be working, you can always shift toward a more overt approach.

> Who in your life is an aware adaptive alpha?
>
> Are you an aware adaptive alpha?
>
> Based on your responses, what change could you make in your next interaction to increase your influence?

Here is a summary chart of all things alpha to help you determine the type of alpha you might be working with and the strength approaches most likely to influence the situation.

The Alpha Matrix

ON
POINT
ADVISING

	Nonadaptive	Adaptive
Aware of Self and Impact on Others	**Taps into Others' Emotional Triggers** Often perceived as a bully Decreases engagement Wins in short term Relies on dominant strength Aaron Rodgers *The Office*: Jan, Angela, Stanley Strength Style to Use: 1) Overt or 2) Subtle Strength	**Versatile** High influence quotient Patient and strategic Manages ego Leverages overt and Subtle Strength Kelly Ripa, Warren Buffett *The Office*: Jim, Karen Strength Style to Use: 1) Overt or 2) Subtle Strength
Unaware of Self and Impact on Others	**Reacts to Triggers** Relies on what comes to mind Often perceived as a bully and narcissist Jack Nicholson in *A Few Good Men* *The Office*: Michael Scott, Meredith Strength Style to Use: 1) Subtle or 2) Overt Strength	**Responds to Triggers** Relies on what comes to mind Tom Cruise *The Office*: Andy Strength Style to Use: 1) Subtle or 2) Overt Strength

Figure 2.1. The Alpha Matrix

Navigating Narcissists

Narcissism is a popular topic today and for good reason. Dealing with narcissists can be one of the most challenging aspects of life and work. They don't even have to be in positions of power. They create dysfunction wherever they go, and more time and emotional energy is focused on their negative impact at work than on the work itself. Just as it's important to know which kind of alpha you're interacting with, I also want you to be able to recognize when you might be interacting with a narcissist. Much like bullies, all narcissists are alphas, but by no means are all alphas narcissists, nor do they necessarily demonstrate narcissistic tendencies.

What is narcissism, exactly? As my close friend Pete Theodorakos tells me, everything started with the Greeks. According to WebMD, the word *narcissist* comes from a Greek myth in which a handsome young man named Narcissus sees his own reflection in a pool of water and falls in love with it.[12]

Narcissistic personality disorder is a diagnosable condition, but many people behave like narcissists yet do not have narcissistic personality disorder. Below is an overview of narcissistic tendencies, based on WebMD as well as my experience in business, sport, and healthcare.

Characteristics of narcissists usually include the following:
- Are able to manipulate others
- Have an inflated sense of self
- Are insecure at the core
- Lack empathy
- Do not value others
- Disregard others' point of view

They might act in the following ways:
- Struggle to maintain relationships

- Take advantage of others' good nature
- Have a high need for attention and admiration
- Have a "me first" mindset
- Frustrate and upset others often
- Talk about themselves a lot
- Overestimate their talents and achievements
- Think they are more special than others
- Set goals that are not achievable
- Take credit for wins and blame others for losses
- Are moody
- Discount the experience of others
- Disengage from people who can't do something for them
- Are takers and not givers unless it benefits them
- Often work in roles that have a lot of positional power
- Make others lose when they win
- Have fantasies of acquiring great wealth and power
- Appear to have high self-esteem, but actually have low self-esteem

In conversations and relationships, narcissists often exhibit the following tendencies:

- Are emotionally reactive
- Easily get hurt when someone gives them feedback or disagrees with them (also called narcissistic injury)
- Make excuses for flaws
- Play the victim
- Do not take ownership
- Manipulate others
- Identify people's weaknesses and prey on them
- Convince people of things that are not true
- Are overly competitive

- Only engage with people they perceive to be on their level
- Shame others
- Talk over people

As you read that list, you might have wondered, *Am I a narcissist?* The truth is all of us might notice these characteristics from time to time. The difference between normal human behavior and narcissistic behavior is that narcissists exhibit these behaviors as consistent character patterns. These characteristics are not situational but at the core of who they are.

The more narcissistic characteristics a person consistently displays over time, the more likely it is they are a narcissist.

Why is it important to know if you are interacting with a narcissist? Because if you want to influence a narcissist, you will need to manage your expectations and be very intentional about the strength style you use. The more narcissistic elements someone has, the more difficult it is to influence them.[13]

When working with narcissists in a therapeutic setting, I found the number one success factor was a strong working relationship. They needed to trust me before they took advice from me. By the way, the same holds true when we think about influencing alphas: build the relationship and you will build influence.

However, the probability of changing a narcissist's behavior in a work setting is very low. In these situations, it's a matter of protecting yourself and others.

The problem is that narcissists' Value-Based Power is overfocused on self, which means they tend to focus on *manipulation* rather than *influence*. While influence can benefit an individual, it is not always solely focused on personal gain and can often include win/win scenarios. Manipulation, on the other hand, is about one thing: getting what you want regardless of the cost. Manipulation also often involves doing something *to* people to get your desired result, such as intimidation, coercion, or intentionally tapping into people's triggers.

For this reason, if you are working with a narcissist, consider shifting your goal from trying to influence them to figuring out *if* you are able to influence the situation—or if you need to leave the situation. Of course, leaving is rarely easy to do, but if you or others are suffering, something needs to change.

BullyProof Strategy #2: Identify the Alpha

1. When you're having trouble influencing someone in a positive way, review the Alpha Quiz. Is this person an alpha?

2. If this person is an alpha, review the four types of alphas on the Alpha Matrix. What type are they?

3. The next time you interact with this person, use one of the recommended strength styles on the Alpha Matrix for that type.

Now that you can recognize alphas and their types more easily, you've probably already realized that using the right strength style in the moment is easier said than done—especially if both you and the alpha are under stress. In the next chapter, we'll discuss the neuroscience of influence so you can more easily leverage Subtle Strength and Value-Based Power even in high-stake situations.

Awareness, Application, and Alliances

What insights did I have in this chapter?

What will I apply and when?

With whom will I share what I learned?

CHAPTER 3

Train Your Brain: The Role of Neuroscience in Influence and Success

"She has no right to undermine my authority. She completely ignored my requests and it's my call. She is not putting our kid first and she needs to know she can't push me around. I'm going to email back and tell her exactly how it is." In this interaction between a divorced couple, the ex-husband had reached his limit and became triggered. He went into a dominant strength style and lost view of the big picture. His reaction of emailing back set up a spiral of dysfunctional behavior and ended up making it even worse for the child involved.

Of course, there are times when someone needs to take a stand, but *how* you take a stand matters. The mistake made here was emotion was high and intention was low, which created a larger challenge than the initial one.

The truth is that when we get reactive, our brain is simply behaving according to design. An important step to becoming BullyProof is to understand how the real bully is sometimes our own brain!

The Neuroscience of Stress Reactions

Daniel Friedland, MD, conscious leadership expert and author of *Leading Well from Within*, makes the point that if we want to lead well in the world, we must learn to lead ourselves first. As he puts it, we must "learn how our brain works to better work our brain"—especially when our brain is under stress.[14]

The Triune Brain

Friedland calls the brain "a multilayered system to meet a hierarchy of needs." He notes that it's helpful to think of our brain as made up of three primary parts: the brain stem, the limbic system, and the prefrontal cortex.

The *brain stem*, also called the reptilian brain because we share these functions with all reptiles and other animals, governs our survival needs, fight-or-flight behaviors, and unconscious movements and habits.

The *limbic system*, also called the mammalian brain because we share these functions with all mammals, governs our primal drives related to sex, bonding, and taking care of our young. It also governs our memory, emotions, and sense of safety. Most notably, the limbic system includes the *amygdala*, which is constantly scanning our environment looking for potential threats based on our memories of past experiences.

If a current situation appears to match a past threat, the amygdala will alert our brain stem and our hypothalamus to begin the fight-or-flight response, often called an *amygdala hijack*, which we will discuss more in chapter 8. The fight-or-flight response is a sympathetic nervous system response that increases our breathing and heart rate, floods our system with adrenaline, norepinephrine, and cortisol to get moving fast, and focuses all our attention on fighting or fleeing the threat.

This response evolved to become a very efficient way to mobilize resources if we're facing a physical threat, but as we'll see in a moment, it is much less helpful if we're facing a psychological threat, such as, say, being yelled at by our supervisor.

The *neocortex,* also called the neomammalian brain, is our source of conscious awareness, conscious leadership, and high performance. It governs our ability to perceive the world accurately, strategize, make good decisions, and connect well with others. In particular, it contains our prefrontal cortex, which helps with emotional regulation; integrates information from our insular cortex, which includes our "heart intelligence" and "gut instinct"; and coordinates executive function, willpower, and the ability to stand outside our thoughts and feelings and observe them (what is often called "mindfulness").

Friedland emphasizes that no part of the brain is less valuable than the other; in fact, they all work together to meet a hierarchy of needs, to use Abraham Maslow's term. Friedland simplifies Maslow's hierarchy of needs to three layers—safety, love and belonging, and significance—and notes that the three parts of the brain align with these three categories of needs: the brain stem with safety, the limbic system with love and belonging, and the neocortex with significance.

Redefining Stress

As we said previously, the amygdala is constantly scanning for potential threats, and when it identifies one, it signals the brain stem and hypothalamus to initiate the fight-or-flight response. Because we are now in survival mode, cut off from our neocortex and our best decision-making abilities, we can get stuck in what Friedland calls a *cycle of reactivity*, which is the cycle of fight/flight, trigger, fight/flight, trigger, and which results in the kind of behavior we saw from the ex-husband above.

Not only does the fight-or-flight response cut us off from our best decision-making abilities, but increased cortisol, adrenaline, and norepinephrine also increases long-term health risks, so it's not a response we want to be in very often, unless it's truly a matter of life or death.

The good news is that we have other responses available to us besides this "threat" response.

According to Friedland, what determines whether our fight-or-flight response is triggered is one simple equation: whether we believe the demands on us are exceeding our resources.

If we believe our demands exceed our resources, the fight-or-flight response is triggered and we enter a cycle of reactivity, low performance, and a decreased ability to leverage our Value-Based Power.

If we believe our resources exceed our demands, even in a time of great demand, our fight-or-flight response is not triggered, which means we can enter what Friedland calls a *cycle of creativity*, with full access to our best faculties and an increased ability to fully use our Value-Based Power to create *cycles of giving and receiving*.

We often interpret any feeling of stress as a sign we can't handle a situation, and it is, therefore, a threat. But Kelly McGonigal, health psychologist and author of the *Upside of Stress*, offers a different definition of stress.

"Stress is what arises when something you care about is at stake."[15]

This definition of stress means our experience of stress is neither bad nor good; it's simply energy. In other words, we can allow the energy of stress to bully us and take us down, or we can leverage stress as an asset to fuel our pursuit of what matters most to us.

If we interpret stress as energy to give us the resources we need, stress is no longer interpreted as a threat, and all of a sudden two other responses become available to us: (1) the *challenge response*, where we realize that demands are high but we are ready to rise to the occasion, and (2) the *tend-and-befriend response*, where we reach out to others for increased resources and social support.

Research has identified that both of these stress responses result in their own set of automatic responses.

The challenge response is also a sympathetic nervous system response, and it releases adrenaline, norepinephrine, and cortisol, just like the threat response. The difference is that it releases them in a way that mimics aerobic exercise and improves performance, resulting in better focus, better energy utilization, and better health effects. In addition, it also releases DHEA, and the resulting proportion of DHEA and cortisol has been associated with better problem-solving, greater focus, increased recovery from trauma, better athletic performance, and a number of other instances of improved performance.[16]

The tend-and-befriend response increases the production of oxytocin, known as the love hormone, which helps us feel braver and more trusting and also mitigates against the negative physiological effects of stress.[17]

That means your definition of stress can affect whether stress is a liability or an asset to you.

Choose Your Best Response

How can we lead ourselves well based on the way our brain responds to stress? We can't control what triggers us, but we can control our response. When we realize we are in a reactive state, Friedland recommends three simple steps to shift to a creative state, expand our resources, and leverage stress as energy for what matters most:

1. **Pause**. Pause and take three deep belly breaths, which activates your parasympathetic nervous system and calms you down.

2. **Notice**. Become mindfully aware of your sensations, thoughts, and feelings.

3. **Choose**. Choose your best response. When it comes to responding well to psychological demands, the threat response is a sledgehammer, says Friedland. To increase your resources so your current stress is no longer interpreted as a threat, you can choose the tend-and-befriend response or the challenge response.

The more we train our brain with practices like Pause, Notice, and Choose, the more we remind ourselves that stress is not a threat but an opportunity to increase our resources. And the more we view stress as energy to help us increase our resources, the less often we'll experience bullying behavior as a threat. Instead of entering a cycle of reactivity, we'll be more likely to enter a cycle of creativity, have access to our highest abilities, and create cycles of giving and receiving to shift the culture around us.

> ## Shift from a Reactive State to an Intentional State
> - Practice Pause, Notice, and Choose.
> - Use active relaxation techniques, such as deep breathing or imagery, to calm your trigger points.
> - Catch and release. Game fishers know the art of letting go of what comes their way. You do not need to keep every thought or feeling. Set them free.

Does this approach really work? The best answer is found in Friedland's life. In November 2020, he was diagnosed with stage 4 glioblastoma, a type of brain cancer. As a medical doctor, he knew that type of cancer was considered uncurable and he had just received a terminal diagnosis. Because it was during the pandemic, his wife and two boys were unable to be with him in the hospital, so he received the diagnosis alone. After he received the news, he was lying in a hospital bed. As he tells the story, he asked himself, "What do I do? How did this happen?" and felt himself cycle into fear and stress. In the midst of this reactive cycle, he was able to pause, notice, and choose—and ask a better question: "What matters most now?"

The answer that came to him: "Make every moment count."

The next logical question was, "How?"

His answer: "By living intensely loving relationships."

That "better question" and its series of answers allowed him to shift to a cycle of giving and receiving and allowed him to find love, belonging, meaning, and purpose even in a life-threatening situation. This led him through an upward spiral of growth through his cancer journey. Whenever demands exceeded resources and he found himself in a reactive state, he returned to the question that expanded his resources: What matters most now? Because he had become a master of increasing his resources when needed, especially the resources of loving relationships, he no longer experienced his cancer diagnosis as a threat, but as an opportunity to tend and befriend and to rise to meet a challenge, increasing his sense of significance and purpose.

This choice to live a loving life led him and his family to share their journey through a YouTube channel called Living Well from Within, created to help encourage and support others facing massive challenges, especially during the pandemic. Although Friedland passed away on October 30, 2021, his work lives on through his book, his YouTube channel, and those who have been inspired by his story of living a loving life and leading well from within.

In fact, thanks to our mutual editor Amanda Rooker, I was planning on interviewing him for this book. Amanda saw many similar themes in our work and thought it would be a good connection. Unfortunately, Dr. Friedland passed away before we could meet, but I am honored to include his work here and continue his legacy.

The Neuroscience of Influence

When you can shift from a reactive state to a creative state, you have far more resources available to you. Instead of being a bully, your brain can become more of an ally.

The same is true for others. If you can help them avoid entering a reactive state, they will be more open to your influence. As an added bonus, they also become better able to access their best internal resources and highest levels of performance.

Research supports this idea. For example, when seeking to influence others in a coaching relationship, researchers Richard Boyatzis and Anthony Jack found through brain imaging that "coaching with compassion," or coaching with a focus on the client's positive vision of the future, "activates networks and regions of the brain that are associated with engagement, motivation, stress regulation, and parasympathetic modulation."[18] In contrast, "coaching for compliance," or coaching with a focus on the client's weaknesses, activated networks and regions of the brain associated with "SNS [sympathetic nervous system] activity, self-trait attribution, and negative affect."[19]

So if you want to influence someone, you'll have more success if you start by asking them about their positive vision of the future rather than pointing out what they're not doing. This approach creates openness to new ideas, motivation, and a willingness to connect with you, while the tougher approach can trigger a reactive state and leave them unable to access those abilities they need to do what is needed.

Paul J. Zak's neuromanagement research has established that the brain chemical oxytocin is the key to prosocial behaviors in an organization. He summarizes his findings as follows: "In a more than decade's worth of human experiments in my laboratory and at numerous field sites, my colleagues and I have shown that OT [oxytocin] is the biological basis for the Golden Rule: If you treat me well, my brain will synthesize OT and this will motivate me to reciprocate."[20]

According to Zak's research, oxytocin is produced quickly after positive social interactions and shuts down during periods of stress. Oxytocin is associated with increased compassion, empathy, and cooperation, all of which contribute to more efficient teamwork and higher performance.[21] Zak offers a model for creating a high-trust culture that increases the likelihood of oxytocin release within team members using the acronym OXYTOCIN: Ovation (public praise), eXpectation (setting meaningful challenges), Yield (allowing colleagues to decide how to complete a task), Transfer (allowing colleagues to choose projects to work on), Openness (sharing information freely), Caring, Invest (in colleagues' holistic growth), and Natural (when leaders are authentic and vulnerable).[22]

The work of cognitive neuroscience professor Tali Sharot, author of *The Influential Mind: What the Brain Reveals About Our Power to Change Others*, also supports the idea that fear negatively impacts our ability to be influenced. According to Sharot, when stressed, our brains tend to prioritize negative messages over positive messages, which affects our ability to be influenced. Also, according to the "backfire effect," if someone has a strong belief and you're trying to influence them with facts, that person will double down on their beliefs and work even harder to debunk the facts or ignore them.

So how can we influence people effectively? We can begin with a positive message instead of a negative one. Stress studies show that our brains are better at encoding hopeful information than encoding information that implies things are going to get worse.

More specifically, according to Sharot, "inducing hope is more likely to induce action, while inducing fear is more likely to induce inaction."[23] In one experiment, she and her colleagues asked participants either to press a button to get a dollar, or press a button to avoid losing a dollar. They found participants more quickly and accurately pushed the button to receive the reward versus pushing the button to avoid a loss. Conversely, when participants were asked to not do anything to receive a dollar and not do anything to avoid losing a dollar, they more frequently chose not doing anything to avoid losing a dollar.

So if you want to influence someone to do something, focus on the positive results of doing it instead of the negative results of *not* doing it, which is likely to induce inaction.[24]

The bottom line is that using the tend-and-befriend response in stressful situations not only helps us stay out of a reactive state and in our most responsive and open state, it helps our colleagues do the same. When you want to influence someone, being kind and treating them well increases the likelihood they'll be open to what you have to say.

The Brain Creates Shortcuts

Even when it's not stressed, the brain tends to be lazy and has a need to be efficient. That means it tends to create shortcuts, which include automatic responses to common situations. In fact, 40 to 80 percent of what we do every day is automatic, uninfluenced by new or problem-solving thoughts in the moment.[25]

According to Wray Herbert, author of *On Second Thought*, it takes four to seven repetitions to form the start of a shortcut.[26] In some cases, these shortcuts support us, such as when we go on autopilot when riding a bicycle or driving to work. But very often they don't support us, such as when we automatically judge people or get triggered by certain words or events.

One type of shortcut is *cognitive bias*. The backfire effect, where we tend to strengthen our belief when it's been challenged (mentioned earlier in connection with Tali Sharot's work), is one type of cognitive bias, but there are many other cognitive biases that save us the "work" of learning something new.

Here are just a few common ones:

- Confirmation bias: Looking for information that confirms our own ideas or beliefs.
- In-group and out-group bias: Unfairly favoring members in a group we identify with and tending to believe the worst of members outside that group. We can identify with political groups, gender, race, ethnicity, nation, reli-

gion, food beliefs, school, sports teams, and many other types of groups. See chapter 10 for much more about group identity and in-group and out-group bias.

- Recency bias: The tendency to believe situations that have happened recently are more likely to occur than events that happened in the more distant past.
- Ageism: Favoring youth over age.
- Gender bias: According to the American Psychological Association, "any one of a variety of stereotypical beliefs about individuals on the basis of their sex, particularly as related to the differential treatment of females and males."[27]
- Fundamental attribution error: When we find reasons to excuse our failures but blame others for their failures.
- Status bias: The tendency not to challenge a source if it is associated with a well-known institution.

Which cognitive biases do you notice in yourself? In others?

Clichés are another type of shortcut. In American culture, we have a tendency to use clichés to ease tension or make people feel better. I have noticed that not only are clichés not helpful, they may actually do harm. At best they make the person who says them feel better because they had something to say. At worst they do damage because they tend to encourage a victim mentality rather than an ownership mentality and disempower the person who may be in a tough spot.

Which of these clichés have you used or heard others use?

- Everything happens for a reason.

- It was meant to be.
- We are only presented with what we can handle.
- Time heals all wounds.
- It is what it is.
- What doesn't kill you makes you stronger.

Energy and inertia are powerful. If we set our minds in a direction, unless we intentionally redirect it, we will continue to follow the same narrative.

> Do you rely on certain clichés? What types of situations or truths might they be protecting you from?

I have also noticed that the more pressure we experience, the less we are aware of acting on our biases—and the more we double down on them. In fact, it's estimated that our brains are automatically running approximately one hundred unhelpful shortcuts.[28] It's important to be aware that when our brain reacts, it might be due to a shortcut that may or may not serve us.

Can Our Brains Really Change?

If our brains are wired to overreact and create unhelpful shortcuts, is there anything we can do about it? Is it possible to train our brain to react less?

In recent years, the term *neuroplasticity* has become popular, even in everyday conversation. Neuroplasticity refers to the relatively recent discovery that our brains are not fixed at adulthood but can change and develop over time.

Many popular speakers and leaders interpret this idea very broadly, assuming neuroplasticity means we can change everything about our brain.

Science is one of the purest processes we have. Unfortunately, it can also be misused to make generalizations and misguide people. Because science is a process rather than an event, what we know today about our brains and influence may evolve. But there are findings that support the idea of neuroplasticity.

Ken Nowack is a well-respected consulting psychologist and researcher who often challenges the tendency to oversimplify and overapply research conclusions. He and his colleague Dan Radecki note that neuroplasticity does have a scientific basis, but with the following limitations:

- Use it and improve it: Using specific brain areas can enhance plasticity within that brain region.
- Use it or lose it: Failure to activate certain brain functions causes loss.
- Specificity matters: The nature of the behavior dictates neuroplasticity.
- Repetition matters: Repetition of newly learned or relearned behavior is required for lasting neural changes.
- Difficulty and challenge matters: Sufficient intensity facilitates plasticity.
- Salience matters: Emotion, motivation, and attention are all important factors for neuroplasticity.
- Age matters: Training induced plasticity occurs more readily in younger brains.
- Drivers matter: Some activities coupled with learning and memory facilitate greater neuroplasticity (e.g., physical activity/exercise and sleep).[29]

What I take from this list is that it is possible to change our brain within certain parameters.

Years ago I took pilot lessons. Spoiler alert: I didn't finish because I cut my hand, had to have surgery, and had to take a break because I couldn't hold the yoke properly. Then life happened, and I haven't gotten back to it yet. I learned very early on that clarity and intention are foundational to keeping your mind open to learning. Every time we changed who was in charge of the controls, we followed a three-step process. First the instructor would say, "You have the controls." Then I would say, "I have the controls." Finally the instructor would say, "You have the controls." This process left no chance for miscommunication and there was absolute clarity about who was in control.

I start many presentations and conversations by telling this story and letting people know they have the controls for their mind. If we're flying a plane in the middle of a storm, a gust of wind may cause the plane to go off course. But we don't have to allow the wind to control the plane. We have the controls, so we can guide the plane back on course.

The same is true for our mind. Something may happen to trigger a threat response, bias, or automatic shortcuts, but we don't have to let those influence control our thinking or our behavior. We have the controls. Thanks to neuroplasticity, there are even things we can do to train our brain to stay on course more easily.

Here are some ways researchers suggest we can train our brain.

According to Robert Eichenger, our brain has two primary operating systems: automatic and diplomatic.

- The reporter (automatic) narrates and tells stories all day long. The reporter writes scripts that feel like facts and will automatically move you in a direction unless you edit the story.

- The editor (diplomatic) has the choice to talk to the reporter and change the story.

Eichenger says we have about 0.5 seconds to adjust and train our brain to go in the correct direction rather than the lazy direction. We can take the controls and use our editor to create new habits in our brain.[30]

Based on their study of top performers, researchers K. Anders Ericsson, Michael J. Prietula, and Edward T. Cokely deduced that expertise was a result of practice, not innate ability. But it wasn't just any practice; it was what they called *deliberate practice*. Deliberate practice means practicing what you *don't* know how to do with intentional focus in order to improve what you want to improve.[31]

According to Ericsson, Prietula, and Cokely,

> The journey to truly superior performance is neither for the faint of heart nor for the impatient. The development of genuine expertise requires struggle, sacrifice, and honest, often painful self-assessment. There are no shortcuts. It will take you at least a decade to achieve expertise, and you will need to invest that time wisely, by engaging in "deliberate" practice—practice that focuses on tasks beyond your current level of competence and comfort.[32]

This kind of deliberate practice also happens to align within Nowack and Radecki's definition of neuroplasticity: it involves specificity, repetition, difficulty, and attention.

So when you find yourself in a reactive state, let your editor take the controls and practice shifting to a more intentional state. When you notice yourself relying on shortcuts or cognitive biases, use deliberate practice to train your brain to do what you don't normally do, such as asking questions or pausing before taking action.

BullyProof Strategy #3: Train Your Brain

1. Recognize how your brain can bully you through stress reactions, shortcuts, and biases.
2. Use deliberate practice to train your brain to shift from a reactive or biased state to a more intentional state.
3. To avoid triggering the bully in others, influence with empathy and hope rather than pressure or fear.

It takes intention to make an impact. You can train your brain to react less and influence more. It just takes time to become an effective electrician. After all, how long did it take you to be effective in your current role?

The way our brain works is something that unites us. Now that you have some tools to train your own brain, in the remainder of Part 1 you'll learn specific strategies aligned with this neuroscience to more effectively influence others.

Awareness, Application, and Alliances

What insights did I have in this chapter?

What will I apply and when?

With whom will I share what I learned?

CHAPTER 4

Motivational Currency: The Coins of Influence and Inclusion

"He's a driver and too operationally focused. He is intimidating and a pure alpha. I don't think he is going to be able to lead our people."

That was the main message I got about an executive in a technology company I was asked to advise. Let's call him George. When "intimidating alpha" is someone's brand, you can bet people's reactive states are being triggered. As a result, it is difficult to get people to feel engaged and want to collaborate. Even worse, it can decrease productivity and lead to dysfunction.

Whenever there is a negative narrative around someone, there is often a story behind that narrative. I set out to find it before I made any judgments about George for myself.

In my initial conversations with George, I could tell he was a person of high character and cared about people. I began to shadow him at work to learn more about why he was perceived as operational and not people focused. I could sense there was a mismatch between George's intentions and his impact.

There was a lot of pressure from the CEO and other executives to increase sales, and they put it on George to get results through people. This resulted in George being very task focused because he knew what behaviors lead to sales success. But why were people not seeing what I saw, which was that he found meaning in his work and cared about people? The answer was clear: George was not aware of his Motivational Currency® profile and what drove the people around him.

Motivation Matters

"How do we keep people motivated with all of this uncertainty and fear?" This is a question I continue to get asked by clients, especially during tough times. The answer is simple but not easy. I believe that motivation is personal and needs to come from within. What's needed is a shift from trying to motivate people to inviting people to be motivated.

We consistently confuse motivation with inspiration. Inspiration is often short term. For example, inspiration is what you experience after hearing a feel-good speech. Gifted speakers tap into your emotions and tell stories that make you feel positive and inspired, but it usually doesn't last.

We can also confuse a lack of productivity with a lack of motivation. We often ask ourselves why we do some things quickly and easily but lack motivation for others. Most of us are familiar with Stephen Covey's concept of urgent versus important tasks from his book *The 7 Habits of Highly Effective People*. We tend to do what feels "urgent," such as a time-sensitive need from our colleague, but put off the "important" tasks, like our exercise routine, which represent what actually matters most to us but don't have specific timelines. When we don't get things done, many of us assume we're simply focused on what's urgent and we just need to work harder to get the "important" done.

While this approach may help with prioritization, it doesn't help with managing your energy and tapping into what makes you tick. If you're noticing a lack of productivity in yourself or others, I'd like to suggest there's more than just urgent versus important at work. What matters most is what *motivates* us.

One way to offset risks, increase engagement, and improve productivity is to shift the way you think about motivation and diversify your approach so you meet people where they are. Think of motivation as the force that drives people. This type of motivation increases engagement and lasts longer than a booster shot of enthusiasm. The way to reach people where they are is to appreciate that people have a variety of motivational drivers and communication styles.

Motivational Currency

If motivation is so important, how can we find out what motivates people and, just as important, what do we do once we know?

There are many theories of motivation, and they can be categorized into two groups: content theories and process theories.

According to content theories of motivation, motivation is driven by wants and needs. These theories include the following:

- Maslow's Hierarchy of Needs
- Alderfer's ERG Theory
- Herzberg's Two-Factor Theory
- McGregor's Theory of X and Y
- McClelland's Three Needs Theory
- Deci's Self-Determination Theory

According to process theories, motivation is driven by rational decision-making, where people weigh what they get in return for what they expect. These theories include the following:

- Adam's Equity Theory
- Vroom's Expectancy Theory
- Bandura's Self-Efficacy Theory
- Skinner's Reinforcement Theory
- Locke's Goal-Setting Theory[33]

In his textbook *Human Motivation*, Harvard psychologist David McClelland looked at social motives and what drives our behavior internally.[34] His work led to my development of Motivational Currency, which is a simple approach to reading and leading based on an appreciation of what drives each individual person.[35] The core four motivators are Performance, People, Power, and Purpose.

Motivational Currency is a combination of both content and process theories of motivation: it combines pursuing an individual's wants and needs with rational decision-making. With virtual interactions here to stay, it's even more important to increase the probability of successfully influencing people by suspending your initial instinct and leading with intention. Most conflict is a result of different motivators and style rather than substance.

As much as we wish it were as simple as a one-size-fits-all solution, when it comes to motivation and much of psychology, people are unique, and we take action based on our personalities, previous experiences, and current situation. Therefore, although most people will have a primary motivator, it is often the case that people have multiple motivators. Someone can be highly motivated and driven by Performance as much as they are by People. The stronger your motivators are in one area, the easier it is for you to make decisions and the more challenging it is to manage your impulses.

Below are descriptions of the four motivators presented in an intuitive and straightforward way. Your goal is to *recognize, read,* and *lead*:

- *Recognize* what your strongest and weakest motivators are.
- *Read* what the motivators are for others.
- *Lead* with intention so you can adapt your approach to align with other peoples' motivators quickly and effectively.

One of my many pet peeves is when psychologists or academics try to force people into a box or a color code. Our personalities have more to them than a one-size-fits-all approach can address. One unique aspect of this framework is that while most people have a primary motivator, people can be high, medium, or low for any of the four motivators. In other words, just because you are high on one motivator doesn't mean you need to be low on another.

Performance

The Performance motivator is about results. Individuals driven by performance want to get things done. They pride themselves on not just completing tasks but excelling. A person with a drive for performance thrives on meeting challenges and exceeding standards. They are often fast-paced, direct, and focused on outcomes. Performance-driven people are not afraid to challenge the status quo and expect others to have as much drive as they do.

Often alphas score at the extreme on the Performance motivator. This is neither good nor bad. What matters more is what type of alpha they are. If they are an aware adaptive alpha, they will be skilled at managing themselves and aware of their impact on others. The challenges come when the alpha isn't aware and isn't adaptive. Another challenging factor is if the alpha does not have an elevated People or Purpose motivator to balance out the strong preference to drive and get results.

I see this frequently in highly results-oriented roles where there are clear targets, such as sales. A person who has a very strong Performance motivator and low People and Purpose motivators can be at risk at getting results at all costs. Often they can be perceived as self-focused, not team players, and people who don't value others.

Contrast this with someone who has a high Performance motivator and a high People motivator. The People motivator balances out the focus on driving results. This person can still get results, but the way they go about it will likely be different. People with this motivation profile focus on a balance between results and relationships, and they are often skilled at getting results through collaboration.

This in no way suggests that people with a high Performance motivator can't be effective leaders or influencers. Again, what is important is a person's ability to be aware and adapt. The stronger your motivators are, the more challenging it is to adapt, but it can be done.

An example of an alpha motivated by Performance is Tom Brady. As the quarterback for the New England Patriots, he had the behaviors of an aware nonadaptive alpha, but since leaving the Patriots, he seems to have evolved to an aware adaptive alpha. He's still a driver and an alpha, but he seems to be engaging more with people and having more fun.

People

The People motivator is about relationships. Individuals driven by the People motivator are most concerned about getting along, teamwork, and collaboration. They are focused on how things impact other people. They tend to have a strong social radar and can read people well. In groups, the People-driven person is often the person who asks a lot of questions, is inclusive, and focuses on getting everyone's opinion. A common descriptor of someone who is People driven is "nice" or "team-oriented."

An example of an alpha with a high People motivator is Duane "The Rock" Johnson. He is a wildly successful actor, businessman, and father of three. He is often seen being a father to his children and is known to be a good collaborator. While we don't know for sure if all these characteristics are true, he has had many public interactions with people where he is clearly enjoying his colleagues and working collaboratively.

Power

The Power motivator is about influence. People motivated by Power put a premium on being persuasive and offering their point of view. They often are effective at providing advice and communicating the importance of brand and reputation. Keep in mind that Power in this context is not necessarily self-focused. Very successful and kind people can have a strong Power motivator. For example, the Dalai Lama is clearly driven by having an impact and influencing people in a positive direction.

An example of an alpha with a high Power motivator is Anderson Cooper. He often gives his point of view and seeks to influence others.

Purpose

The Purpose motivator is about helping others and contributing to something outside of ourselves. Many Purpose-driven people are motivated by developing others or volunteering and community involvement. They often crave purpose and meaning in their work. They excel at getting people to focus on the greater good and can be tremendous enterprise contributors. They can also get people to think across business silos and think about what is best for the entire group or business rather than individuals or teams.

Oprah Winfrey is the ultimate example of someone who has a strong Purpose motivator. She continues to serve the greater good.

A very common and popular approach to understanding our interpersonal patterns is TRACOM's version of social styles. The basic premise is that we all have a preferred way to interact and communicate with others, and different approaches have a different impact based on who you are interacting with. If you're already familiar with TRACOM's model, Motivational Currency gives us insight into what drives our behaviors beneath the surface. If you'd like a snapshot of how these two frameworks interact, go to https://onpointadvising.com/bullyproof.

Recognize Your Own Motivational Currency

Now that you have a basic understanding of the four motivators, take it a step further and recognize what drives you. Use the image below and take your best guess at what your Motivational Currency profile is. The goal is to deepen your insight so you can be more effective at influencing yourself and others.

Figure 4.1. Motivational Currency Calculator

If you'd like a more in-depth assessment of your Motivational Currency, I invite you to take the Motivational Currency Calculator (MCC) at https://onpointadvising.com/motivational-currency/. The MCC can help you recognize what motivates you, read what motivates others, and lead in a way that is aligned with what motivates others. It can be applied when leading, engaging, or influencing people in any context.

Franz and Jana Wieduwilt of Wieduwilt Kommunikation based in Germany have partnered with me to create a German version of the Motivational Currency Calculator called VIEL Motivation. You can learn more at VIELMotivation.com.

What is your Motivational Currency?

Knowing our motivational currency can also help us be more aware of our tendencies related to Value-Based Power. For example, if you score high on Performance, you will likely focus more on self and organizational ambitions. Consider your Motivational Currency and what it may reveal about your focus on the four areas of Value-Based Power.

Read Others' Motivational Currency

Recognizing the motivators in yourself is the first step. The second step is reading them in others. The better you are at reading people, the better you will be at leading people and adapting. The key to uncovering other people's Motivational Currency is asking good questions. Below is a list of questions and probes to help you pick up on cues.

Sample Questions and Probes to Uncover Motivational Currency in Others

- Tell me about what you currently do at work that inspires you.
- Have you ever been so engaged in a task that you lost track of time? If so, what were you doing?

- What aren't you yet involved in that you would like to be involved in?
- How do you respond when someone doesn't complete a task on time?
- What do you see as your primary function in your role?
- Describe a senior leader you admire. What do they do that you admire?
- What frustrates you the most when trying to motivate someone?
- How do you spend your time outside of work?
- If you could have any career outside of your current career, what would it be and why?
- What percent of your work week do you spend doing what truly motivates you? What do you want to do more of? Less of?
- On a scale of 0 to 10, how effective do you think you are at motivating others?
- What has been the most motivating aspect of the work you do?

As the person answers these questions, look for the following key words, or "coins," that may identify their Motivational Currency, as shown in the following chart.

Coins of Motivational Currency

	Performance	People	Power	Purpose
Descriptors	• Results	• Relationships	• Influence	• Meaning
Motivated by	• Completing tasks • Goals • Challenges	• Teamwork • Getting along • Collaborating	• Persuading • Selling • Branding	• Helping • Values • "Something greater"
Focuses on	• Agendas	• Feelings	• Impressions	• Greater good
Potential Challenges	• Impatience • Trouble listening • Over-ambitious	• Slow results • Overly emotional • Avoiding conflict	• Self-focused • Overly political • Trouble listening	• Not business focused • Impractical • Not time oriented
Tips	• Talk about tasks and timelines • Demonstrate confidence • Get things done • Be quick, be done, be gone	• Talk about relationships • Demonstrate appreciation • Communicate understanding • Be nice, be about the team	• Talk about self • Plant seeds and let them make the call • Talk about their vision and priorities • Be aware of their ambitions	• Talk about values • Connect to meaning • Help without wanting anything in return • Be focused on things that don't directly benefit you

ON POINT ADVISING ©2021 OnPoint Advising

Figure 4.2. Coins of Motivational Currency

Analyzing our data from the Motivational Currency Calculator across industries, we have noticed the following trends: Women rate themselves higher than men on Purpose. Men rate themselves higher on Performance and Power. Men and women have similar ratings for People. Men and women do not differ on their accuracy scores for "Leading," which means identifying the correct communication approach based on someone's primary motivator. However, women tend to have a higher accuracy score related to "Reading," which is how effectively one can pick up on cues and identify someone's primary motivator.

In regard to generations, our team was surprised to learn that Millennials have more similar motivation profiles to Baby Boomers than Generation X. Millennials rate themselves highest on Power and Purpose. Generation X rates themselves highest on Performance. All generations rate themselves similarly on People. Generation X scores highest on "Reading."

Lead Others with Motivational Currency

Once you recognize what drives you and read what drives others, the next step is to *lead* others by adapting your approach based on the other person's motivators.

For example, when you identify an alpha who has a very strong Performance drive, don't take it personally if they are constantly driving toward results and focusing on tasks. Start with speaking their language and letting them know you value the importance of achieving results and getting things done. Based on what you learned in chapter 3, you know that starting with what someone wants to accomplish rather than what they're doing wrong keeps them open to influence and out of a reactive state. Also, by first aligning with their strong Performance motivator, they will view you as someone with credibility and therefore you will have more influence.

For a detailed chart to help you read others' motivators and lead based on all four Motivational Currency motivators, go to https://onpointadvising.com/bullyproof.

The more you pay attention to what motivates people, the more likely you are to engage people and, therefore, be more effective at influencing them. One way to make this a positive habit is to take ten minutes before important meetings or conversations and complete a Motivation Map. We know that starting a conversation or meeting well is a strong predictor of success. The Motivation Map below will give you a structured approach to assessing Motivational Currency and adapting your style. An editable version is available at https://onpointadvising.com/bullyproof/.

Motivation Map

Person/Topic	Performance	People	Power	Purpose
My MC Rating (High, Med., Low)				
Name of Person and Rating (High, Med., Low)				
Cues/Data				
What do I need to ask?				
How can I adapt to align with their MC?				
How will I start the conversation?				
How can I help this person?				
How can this person help me?				

ON POINT ADVISING ©2021 OnPoint Advising

Figure 4.3. The Motivation Map

Now, back to George and how Motivational Currency can help him with the perception that he is an "intimidating alpha." I wanted to learn more about what motivated George, and I wanted George to learn what his motivation profile was, so we used the MCC to help him to gain insight into how his behavior gets perceived by others.

Here is George's Motivational Currency profile. When we talked through his results, he was not surprised at all. The perception people have of him does not fit what his profile suggests. How could it be that George was perceived as such a driver if he had a high Purpose score and a medium People score?

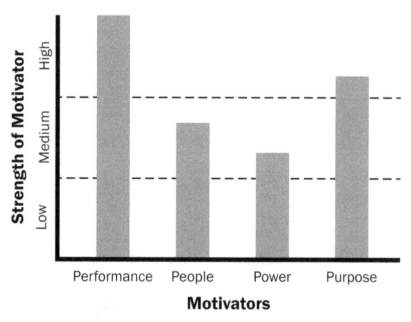

Figure 4.4. George's Motivational Currency Profile

I asked George to explain his profile to me. He said that being results focused, Performance, is clearly his primary motivator. Next, I asked him to explain his high Purpose score. He said that he is determined to build up the business so younger people can create a financially secure life for themselves. He was also motivated by providing for his family and children. I asked him if he ever shared any of this with the employees he works with. You can imagine his answer: "Never."

We discovered one of George's key challenges. When pressure goes up and our reactive state gets triggered, people get pulled by their primary motivator. In George's case, he hits the gas and focuses on tasks, goals, and priorities regardless of the experience it creates for employees—and ignores his other motivators. This also meant his Value-Based Power was limited to self, with limited influence over others, his organization, and society.

To help George adapt by leading with Purpose and paying attention to his impact on people, we created the mantra, "When pressure goes up, hit pause and communicate with Purpose and People in mind."

This mantra buffered the potential unintended consequences of being solely Performance focused. It did not mean George would forget about getting results, quite the opposite. It just meant he would take a long-term approach to influencing people rather than a direct command and control style, which usually results in short-term compliance but long-term resistance.

It wasn't easy, but over time, using tools like the Motivation Map and the mantra, George was able to change from an unaware nonadaptive alpha to an aware adaptive alpha. He simply needed to establish a new habit of adapting to others' Motivational Currencies to counter fifteen years of being rewarded for getting things done. When he became an executive, he needed to learn a different skill set.

So many people are just like George, thinking they are helping people by pushing them to perform. They assume everyone is motivated by Performance like they are. But if they can become more aware of their own Motivational Currency as well as others' and adapt accordingly, they will be able to use all four areas of their Value-Based Power and have an even bigger impact.

The results won't just benefit them but will benefit everyone: when everyone in the organization is getting their motivators met, they'll be less likely to be in a reactive state; more likely to be in a creative, high-performance state; more engaged; make more money; fuel long-term business growth; create meaningful social connections; and find significance and meaning in their work. Everyone wins.

Applications of Motivational Currency

The original intention of developing the Motivational Currency framework was to help people become more effective at influencing others by creating engaging environments where people are invited to be motivated. Over time, the framework has taken on a variety of new uses.

Team Motivation

Teams are always evolving, and we know that the more team members know about one another, the more productive they are. When I work with teams, one of the first things I do is introduce Motivational Currency. I have each team member assess their own Motivational Currency and take their best guess of what each team members' Motivational Currency is. Then we look at their individual and team motivation profile. It allows team members to learn what drives each of them and what they have or lack as a team. For example, if you have a team with a high Power motivator, the team may get results but may be less likely to get credit for them. Or the team may be less likely to provide their points of view or advocate for resources.

Teams that have a diverse range of motivators will naturally have an advantage. And if your team is not diverse, you can either bring on other team members or have individuals ensure all motivators are being represented.

Diversity, Equity, and Inclusion

One Fortune 500 company started using Motivational Currency in their diversity, equity, and inclusion efforts. The approach they use is to focus on appreciating differences in what inspires, engages, and motivates people and paying attention to diversifying their approach when they communicate with others.

Over the years I have had the opportunity to partner with Gagandeep Singh of Hello Excellence. Gagan is a performance and diversity expert and lives in India. His ultimate goal is to end human suffering. We have worked together on training people on Motivational Currency, and I continue to learn from him.

I asked him to share how Motivational Currency can support the important work of Diversity, Equity, and Inclusion (DEI). Here is what Gagan had to say:

I believe that we are all made from the same fabric, not just humans, but all living and nonliving things. We are the threads of a single piece of cloth; every individual is like a single thread which is incomplete without the rest of the threads. Conversely, the fabric is incomplete without each of its individual threads. And because we are all part of the same fabric, I am you and you are me. When you are a part of me, I would do my best to protect you, and your priority is my priority.

Looking at this from an evolutionary psych perspective, people like to be among people who are similar to them, because of familiarity. Familiarity is linked with biological security, and hence we see people similar to us as a part of "our tribe," while those who are different as "others." This us versus them mentality prevents leaders from going out of their comfort zone and achieving their peak potential.

We can use Motivational Currency and the Motivational Currency Calculator (MCC) to overcome this barrier by linking our primary motivators to promote and support DEI. In my case, my primary motivator is Purpose (to enhance people's lives and help them live a good life). By encouraging organizations to promote diversity and inclusion, I am able to create a psychologically safe space where people from different demographics are able to thrive together and reach their peak potential. DEI initiatives also have financial benefits that help organizations become more sustainable and hence continue to enrich people's lives (which again feeds into my purpose). In this way, the MCC helps me become aware of my purpose, which feeds into DEI, which again feeds back into my purpose of helping others. This self-fueling phenomenon helps me unite the threads of the fabric and move universal consciousness forward.

You can see how powerful Gagan's approach to his work can be. Figure 4.5 shows Gagan's Motivational Currency profile.

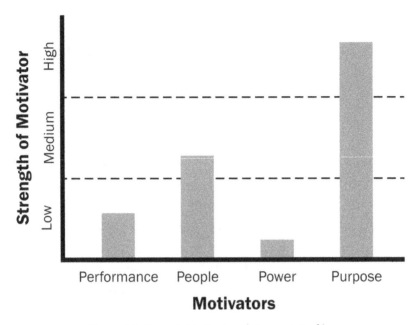

Figure 4.5. Gagan's Motivational Currency Profile

We have had several rich conversations with groups of people about his motivators. Without revealing whose profile it is, one question we ask people is, "Would you want this person on your team?" Most people say no because of the low Performance and Power motivators.

After discussion, we are able to make the point that people with a low Performance motivator can be very successful and get results. Gagan has many gifts, and one of them is his ability to view everything through the lens of Purpose and helping others. This brings him joy and motivation and drives him to get results.

My takeaway from working with Gagan is to be very mindful of the judgments or assessments we make about people's motivators and profiles. While our motivational profiles are important, what's more important is how aware we are and how well we adapt.

Sales

In sales, motivation matters. I know no one better than Anar Desai, vice president of Americas Channels Sales at Palo Alto Networks, at understanding people's Motivational Currency and adapting to the situation. He started out twenty years ago making cold calls, and now he sets the direction and leads a sales team. Anar is someone who has partnered with and influenced some of the most challenging people who have wanted to say no before they knew how he could help their business.

Anar is an ideal person to get perspective from because he is often navigating situations where people are working at different organizations and have different priorities, pressures, and objectives. Somehow he finds a way to understand and deliver. He is a true leader who evidently believes in People, Performance, and not wasting time on things that don't matter.

Anar has no shortage of working with big personalities and strong opinions as he and his team build partnerships, especially with alphas. Large organizations have to work together, despite different business objectives and agendas. Anar and his team are in charge of keeping people on task with priorities. He offered the following thoughts and strategies when working with people who are likely to say no.

When working in sales with large organizations, he suggests these approaches:
1. Build upon common ground outside of the business.
2. Know where the most influential people stand.
3. Understand what motivates each person.
4. Know what the sensitive topics are and bring them up early.

Anar believes that the louder people are, the more you need to be calm and establish the rules of engagement. Find the agreed-upon facts and build trust. He works to have his team create a consistent customer experience regardless of who they are interacting with.

When dealing with the toughest people, Anar recommends not worrying about the alpha. Worry about yourself and know you may not have all the knowledge you need. So, learn. "When people get caught up in proving that they are right, they often go in the wrong direction."

Finally, I asked Anar what his credo is. He offered three points:

1. Be authentic
2. Be creative
3. Be impactful

My favorite thought from Anar related to not getting pulled into the me versus you dynamic. He said, "It's like making an opening argument in court, but no one is listening. That works in a courtroom but not in real life. We have to figure it out without a jury—just me and you and our team."

Anar clearly exemplifies Subtle Strength and pays attention to people's Motivational Currency so he can be intentional and influential.

BullyProof Strategy #4: Recognize, Read, and Lead with Motivational Currency

Choose someone you want to influence or build a greater relationship with and follow these steps.

1. Recognize your Motivational Currency with the Motivational Currency Calculator.

2. Read others' Motivational Currency with the Coins of Motivational Currency.
3. Lead by adapting to align with others' Motivational Currency, using tools like the Motivation Map to support your learning and strategy.

Remember, if you want to verify what drives you, you can take the Motivational Currency Calculator (MCC) at OnPointAdvising.com/MotivationalCurrency. The MCC will give you your profile and additional feedback on how accurate you are at reading others and selecting the correct influence approach to lead them.

Motivational Currency is a framework and approach that is easy to learn and apply. Teams and situations consistently change. Although someone's Motivational Currency profile is relatively stable, life events can have an impact on your motivators. It's good practice to revisit what drives you so you can engage in work that energizes you and be intentional about how you interact with others. And if your role includes influencing alphas, if you lead by communicating with their primary motivator rather than what you are most comfortable with, you decrease the chance for conflict and increase the chance of collaboration and mutual wins.

Awareness, Application, and Alliances

What insights did I have in this chapter?

What will I apply and when?

With whom will I share what I learned?

CHAPTER 5

BRACE for Impact: An Approach for Changing Someone's Mind

As I write this, I am at a Panera Bread. I have my headphones on, and to my left there seems to be a sales meeting playing out. One dominant person and three others are all trying to get their points of view heard. The dominant person keeps talking over and after every person. He has no idea he is demotivating the people around him. He acts as if he is listening, but it's just that—an act. An act that is transforming the conversation into a monologue. His intentions may be positive, but his impact is catastrophic to a collaborative process.

People are smart. They know when someone is listening and when someone is just listening to persuade. This approach comes across as exactly what it is—inauthentic. More often than not, what we call "listening" is simply pausing to allow someone to speak and then picking up where we left off. If you focus on *understanding* rather than listening, you will have a much higher probability of being powerful.

Earlier in the book, we walked through what will *not* change an alpha's mind—using the dominant or submissive strength styles. They are the least effective strength styles because they are both based in the reactive state: the dominant style attacks and submissive avoids. These approaches may seem effective in the short term, but they do harm in the long term.

In our research, we found five facets that increase your chances of changing an alpha's mind, even when they may not be motivated to have their mind changed. There is an art to Subtle Strength, and these five facets will help you gain power and influence without damaging relationships. Just like the facets of a diamond combine to create a beautiful gem, these facets, when combined, can create a valuable collaboration.

The acronym for these five facets is BRACE: Bridging, Respecting, Aligning, Challenging, and Evidence.

BRACE for Impact

When you *brace* for something, you are steady, ready, supported, and anticipating impact. The same goes for when you want to shift someone's thinking. You need to be ready for emotional reactions, hitting triggers, and meeting all reactions with calm confidence.

One of the most challenging parts of life is changing someone else's mind once it's made up, due to our cognitive biases. When we have made a commitment to a certain point of view, our minds tend to find data to reinforce this point of view. And thanks to the backfire effect, the more someone tries to change our mind, the more we try to protect our point of view.

It's especially challenging when the person you're attempting to influence views every disagreement as a threat, which can happen if the person equates "being right" with their self-worth. If you're working with an unaware and/or nonadaptive alpha, they may have no idea why they are triggered; they will simply react. And if their threat response is triggered, you also know from chapter 3 that they will not be very open to outside influence. All their resources will be focused on safety, or, in this case, proving themselves to be right, to restore their sense of self-worth.

One aware adaptive alpha shared with me that from an early age she always had to be—or at least appear to be—the smartest person in the room to feel okay. When she recognized this dynamic as an adult, she shared that she had to do a lot of internal work to break that connection between being right and her self-worth. The good news is that once she did, her threat response was rarely triggered even when someone openly disagreed with her, and she became more open to learning new information.

What's even more challenging than changing a reactive alpha's mind? Changing your *own* mind—especially if an alpha's communication style has sent you into a reactive state. However, just as the aware adaptive alpha was able to train her brain not to react when she received new information, we can also train our brain. As we learned from Dr. Daniel Friedland in chapter 3, when you shift from a reactive state to a more intentional state, you have more resources available to you, even when demands are high.

> What is your go-to practice for shifting out of a reactive state when you get triggered?

So before you put these five facets into action, take control of your mind. If you're in a reactive state, do what you need to do to shift to a more creative state, whether it's using Friedland's Pause, Notice, and Choose technique or another practice that works for you. Say whatever you need to say to yourself to be open.

For me, I say to myself, "learn." If I feel triggered by a dominant personality, I need to get myself in a mindset where I am open to learning from them. I am going to give their point of view a shot because it could be another step toward success or helping others succeed.

When I can shift from a reactive state to an intentional state, I now have full access to my Value-Based Power. I am now free to consider what's best for me, others, my organization, and society, and I gain more clarity about how I want to influence this person.

When it comes to changing someone's mind, listening helps but it's not enough. The challenge of working with a dominant person is that they perceive your listening as agreeing. If you don't change the course of the conversation, not only will you not be able to change their mind, it's likely you'll leave the conversation feeling unheard.

Here are some other common mistakes people make when trying to change someone's mind:

- Trying to influence when emotion is high
- Trying to influence when someone's mind is stuck
- Using the same strategy over and over
- Pushing with evidence alone

The key to changing someone's mind is preventing a reactive state before it starts, since the brain typically shuts down or resists new information when stress arises. That's where the five facets of BRACE come in.

Bridging

When our research team wanted to discover the key factors in changing someone's mind, the most fascinating thing we discovered was that very few people mentioned credibility or positional power. In fact, the number one factor was what we call *bridging*.

Getting someone to go along with your view isn't the same thing as changing someone's mind. No matter how good a listener you are, or how passionately you argue your point of view, changing someone's mind is less about convincing and more about connecting. Bridging means framing the experience for a person so they can see something in a new way.

In our research, we asked survey participants the question:

"When someone is successful at changing your mind, what did they do?"

Here are some examples of how they described bridging.

- "They provided me with facts or metaphors for me to relate to what they are saying. They used examples that everyone goes through or has experienced."
- "Well, one, I have to be willing to change my point of view, but two, they had an argument that made sense to me. I mean, if I think the sky is green, and you hold up a color chart and show me the difference, well, I may consider my opinion may be a bit off."
- "They put their point of view in my perspective."
- "Suggested perspectives I might not have noticed."
- "They opened my eyes to a part of a scenario I've never looked at."
- "They told me about all the positive things that could happen."

The goal of bridging is to connect to the person and subtly open them up to a new experience or way of seeing things. Based on these responses, bridging could include a variety of approaches, such as using metaphors, personal experiences, and real-life examples, that illustrate your point. It's about creating a connection so you can have a real conversation.

Note that this kind of bridge is more like a drawbridge: both sides have to lower their defenses in order to connect.

In fact, bridging is a way to activate the tend-and-befriend response in both parties. Not only are you helping yourself and the other person stay out of a reactive state, you're enabling the release of oxytocin in all parties, so everyone feels more motivated to cooperate and be kind to one another from the beginning. And that means the dominant person will be much less likely to be triggered when you bring in the other facets of Challenges and Evidence later.

Let's use the conversation I overhead at Panera Bread as an example. In that case, the dominant person in that sales meeting was the potential client, and the salesperson wanted to change the client's mind about the product he was selling.

If the dominant person (potential client) automatically started listing all the reasons why their company did not need this type of product, and the salesperson wanted to use the BRACE approach, he could begin with *bridging*. He could agree that the client's concerns are important and then share a real-life example of how this product helped another client solve those very concerns, creating a feeling that he and the client share the common goal of solving the company's problems.

> Think of an alpha you would like to influence. How might you use *bridging* to begin your next interaction?

Respecting

It's very rare that people rise to the top and stay there without respecting others. Plenty of people make a lot of money and treat people very poorly, but based on what I've seen, they burn out or get thrown out. You may recall that the definition of Subtle Strength is intentional influence that uses calm confidence to demonstrate backbone and *respect*. Respecting means valuing someone's insights, managing your own emotions, maintaining your composure, and allowing space for the other person to talk through their perspective.

Here are some examples of how survey respondents described respecting.

- "They let me weigh both sides and come to my own conclusion."
- "They calmly explained why their viewpoint is sensible and did not shove it in my face or act like a child."
- "They gave me time to consider a different viewpoint and didn't rush the conversation."
- "Made me feel important."
- "Gave me time to think about their argument."

To continue with our sales meeting example, if the salesperson shared a real-life scenario and the client openly disagreed with him, the salesperson could *respect* the client by continuing to speak in a calm voice and being patient with him as he processed the new information.

How might you use *respect* with the alpha you want to influence?

Aligning

One of the reasons Warren Buffett has been so successful is he is smart enough to realize that others can add value no matter how smart you are. His consistent approach to engaging others and integrating their insights has served him well. *Aligning* means understanding other people's ambitions and priorities, having a mutual exchange of information, talking about a diversity of ideas, being open to cocreate, continuing to create a connection with the other person, and having collective insights. It primarily has to do with the key skill of *ego agility*, or having "just the right amount of ego" to understand the value of collaborating and bringing in other experts.

Here are some examples of how our survey participants described aligning.

- "Again, when they can make me laugh, I'm more open to their point of view and argument."
- "Listened to me. Allowed for open and honest two-way dialogue. Allowed for brainstorming. Considered compromises where applicable."
- "They give me what I need most out of the situation while getting what they need too. They are aware that there is usually lots of common ground to work with."
- "They simply shared their point of view and didn't make it seem like they were trying to change my mind."
- "Well, they have to be reasonable or at least have considered my point of view. Although, it is rare for me to change my point of view."

If the salesperson wanted to *align* with the client, then instead of continuing to push his own agenda when the client resisted, he could take a step back and consider that maybe he needed to learn more about the client's needs. He could keep an open mind and ask some more questions about the company's priorities and ambitions.

How might you *align* with the alpha you want to influence?

Challenging

A friend who has taught me many lessons over the years and is an example of Subtle Strength is Steve Kincaid, PhD. In a conversation one day, I asked him about working with overpowering people. He wisely responded that many times highly intelligent people test others by *challenging* them to see if they'll challenge back. His wisdom has stayed with me, and I've found it to be a key insight for working with powerful people. It may not even be intentional, but alphas often test by "pushing," or challenging. However, challenging is not the same thing as bullying. First, bullying is caught up in ego, where the bully is insisting that "I'm right and you're wrong." Second, bullying is typically fueled by a personal unmet need or insecurity they are trying to fulfill through you: "Dominating you in this battle makes me feel strong and secure." In other words, bullying is reactive.

In contrast, we found in our research that the key factors of challenging include confidence and assertiveness—also key factors of Subtle Strength. Challenging is about being willing to provide your point of view even if it's different or unpopular. You don't have to be confrontational to challenge someone's thinking. You can say something as simple as, "Would you take a moment to consider an alternative view that may be beneficial to you?"

Here are some examples of how survey respondents described challenging.

- "Their style and confidence which make them unique."
- "They presented me with conflicting facts that challenge my point of view."
- "They first listened to my point of view and used that to try to shape mine."
- "They informed me of new information."
- "They spoke in a consistent manner that illustrated facts but in a confident and gentle way."
- "Showing me new facts that challenge my view."

In our sales meeting example, after aligning with the potential client, the salesperson could use the client's answers to his questions to challenge the client's assumptions about the potential of the product, offering the client new information to consider.

How might you *challenge* the alpha you want to influence?

Evidence

Evidence is the simplest of the five facets: facts are facts. People respond positively to facts that are objective and not based on agendas. For example, one of the biggest problems we have today is that people present arguments that aren't based on logic and truth but just on emotion. Evidence means presenting hard facts, using logic, and being able to back up your statements with data.

Here are some examples of how survey respondents described evidence.

- "They gave me facts."
- "They have to know what they are talking about and be unemotional in their approach."
- "Gave me concrete evidence."
- "They used facts and statistics to reinforce their viewpoint. They don't attack my point of view, just offer reasons for theirs."

Now that the salesperson has a better understanding of the client's needs and has consistently and calmly responded to the client's objections, the salesperson provides objective facts about his product, has data ready to support those facts, and lets the evidence speak for itself.

> How might you use *evidence* with the alpha you want to influence?

In the process of writing this chapter, I wanted to talk to the best of the best in influencing alpha personalities. Immediately I thought of Jason Lenhart, vice president of Engineering & Operations, Direct-to-Consumer Technology at WarnerMedia. I have learned a lot from Jason over the years. I have seen him navigate very challenging situations and a wide range of personalities. He always seems to deliver and make the right decisions when it comes to interacting with people.

I asked Jason if he could share some advice for someone who feels like they are getting bullied at work. He shared that he always guides people to start with finding something everyone would agree on that is verified truth and not an opinion. There is a lot of wisdom in this approach, as it likely de-escalates the emotions involved. Jason also added that he suggests not getting caught up in making it about you and aligning yourself with data. Jason's approach leverages two facets of BRACE, bridging and evidence.

All that Jason shared with me could be put into a course on building credibility and effective influence. He shared one powerful perspective on leading, especially when you are in a position of power: "I don't want to extend my career based on other people's failures." That means even if someone is engaging in bullying behavior, Jason doesn't take it personally and doesn't look to derail or damage that person's career. I have seen this principle in action, and Jason's ability to not get pulled into the political muck is remarkable.

BullyProof Strategy #5: BRACE for Impact

1. *Bridge* to connect with empathy and understanding.
2. *Respect* to allow space for the other person to talk through their perspective.
3. *Align* to find common ground among ambitions and priorities and cocreate collective insights.
4. *Challenge* to share your point of view with confidence and assertiveness.
5. Use *evidence* to back up your statements with data.

Although most of the time you'll want to start with bridging, it's the combination of all five facets that increases your Value-Based Power and your likelihood of changing someone's mind. It's helpful to be able to leverage all of them and to be intentional about which facet you choose. Different people and different situations will require different facets. Be mindful not to get stuck only using the facet you are most comfortable with or that comes most easily. With repeated practice, all of them can be learned, and you will become more successful at influencing others—even alphas.

Awareness, Application, and Alliances

What insights did I have in this chapter?

What will I apply and when?

With whom will I share what I learned?

CHAPTER 6

Defuse the Bomb: Making DEALS with Alphas

We all get put into difficult situations that require us to be our best when things are at their worst. When an alpha gets triggered, it can feel like a bomb went off. I have developed a niche in working in challenging situations, but in this case, I decided to go straight to the experts: people in military special forces who literally need to defuse bombs and influence people when they don't want to be influenced.

Defusing a bomb is just a tad easier when it's a bully than when it's an actual explosive device. I had the honor of talking with Jonny Walker, an Explosive Ordinance Disposal (EOD) team leader who has served tours in Afghanistan, Kuwait, and in the United States. As you might have guessed, people in the EOD are in charge of discovering, disarming, and disposing of bombs, such as when the President of the United States is traveling and needs to ensure the area is safe and free of explosive devices.

I could tell immediately I was talking with someone who was built differently than most and had tremendous mental focus and discipline. I wanted to get his perspective on the approach he takes when he is called out to an active bomb situation as well as his thoughts on how to influence alpha personalities who are potential bullies. Remarkably, there are many parallels: both approaches put a premium on preparation, mindset, and skill set.

We can all imagine the courage it would take for someone to walk up to a potentially live bomb. Although a bomb is an actual physical threat, the experience of walking up to a bully may also elicit fear and hesitancy, both of which can throw your focus off.

Jonny explained to me that a strong mindset and strong skill set are key to his success and keeping safe. He said that everyone in EOD knows that when they go out on a call, they may not return home, which makes your approach to interacting with explosive devices critical. He shared that they use a strategy called the *OODA loop* to stay safe and get the job done. OODA stands for orient, observe, decide, and act.

Jonny told me about the history of the OODA loop. It was a strategy that a World War I ace pilot used, and this pilot never got shot down and always engaged the enemy before they had a chance to engage him. Jonny added that in EOD, you can get called out to crazy situations and a lot of uncertainty. Therefore, not only do you need to have confidence in your process, you need to make OODA a subconscious habit, because it will help you take the correct actions quickly to keep yourself and others safe. The reason it's called the OODA "loop" is because you continue to repeat this process until the job is done.

I asked Jonny to go into more detail about what he does when he encounters a device that might be explosive. I was wondering if his process might have some parallels to interacting with certain types of alphas.

This is what Jonny had to say:

> When I arrive, I ask myself, "Are we safe? Am I safe?" Once everyone is safe, we need figure out if I am moving forward remotely, or I am physically walking up to the device. Then we figure out what the device is. We treat all devices as if they are armed. You literally think through how this device could kill you and how you can keep it from killing you or others. Some things are simple to diagnose. For example, if the device is out of its tube, it's armed. Then I decide if I can move it or can a higher-order detonation occur.

I was very interested in what Jonny does when something goes wrong and a device goes off. He didn't initially understand my question. "Do you mean when we intentionally set something off?" he asked.

"No, I mean when you think a device isn't going to go off and it does," I answered.

What I gathered was that a bomb accidently going off was very rare because their preparation, process, and information is so calculated and accurate. Jonny eventually said, "It may seem very chaotic, but it's very controlled."

Jonny's confidence in his approach was unwavering. I then asked him if he saw commonalities between defusing bombs and interacting with dominant personalities. He said that not only did he see commonalities, but he actually enjoyed working with these types of people. Big surprise, right?

Jonny shared the following story:

I got called out to check on mortars. I found six or seven mortars that were near three hundred people in a battalion. I knew I needed to get them out of the ground. I treated them as dangerous pipe explosives even though I knew some may not be dangerous. I made the call to ask for airspace to shut down the units and clear the area.

At first things were going as planned, and then the COG [Commander of Operations Group], a powerful person with a strong personality, disagreed and asked if they could just put out a bubble and push people out a certain distance. Here is how the conversation went:

COG: Let's just clear some space and put out a bubble.

Jonny: I can see why we'd want to do that. Can you tell me how far the frags will go?

COG: I don't know, but you have to find a different way than shutting things down and clearing the area.

Jonny: Okay. Then I will carry them out of the area myself to keep people safe.

COG: No, you can't do that.

Jonny: Sir, respectfully, I don't want this to come across the wrong way. I was asked to come out here because I am EOD and because I have deep expertise. While you are in charge, I am also in charge, especially when it comes to the mortars. The choices are, I either clear the area now and blow them up, or I walk them out.

COG: Okay. Go ahead and do what you need to.

Jonny went on to share that after everything was completed, the COG called for him. The COG said, "You know, I appreciate what you are doing and what you did for us. Well done. Appreciate you being straight forward. I'd like to give you this coin," a military custom that represented a tangible memento of Jonny's excellence in service.

In this situation Jonny took a risk, but he kept his focus on safety and trusted his training. I asked Jonny what made that interaction with a powerful and dominant person successful. He said that he didn't get pulled into an ego battle and also didn't back down. We can see how Jonny worked to deescalate the situation while communicating through calm confidence and demonstrating both respect and backbone.

This approach is very similar to how we want to interact with nonadaptive unaware alphas and bullies. We want to know what can set them off, take precautions to defuse the explosive, and keep ourselves and others safe.

Jonny shared with me that people don't often admit their mistakes, but doing so is critical to learning so you can prevent future disasters. He embraces the philosophy of realizing he knows a lot but he doesn't know everything and has an open mindset. I would say that Jonny, someone willing to take charge at any moment, demonstrates awareness and adaptability.

"The best part about the EOD force," Jonny said, "is it's all volunteer and people can get out if they want to." Jonny went on to tell me he has no plans of getting out anytime soon and if a time comes when he no longer enjoys it, he'll get out. Let's just say I'm grateful for people like Jonny, other service members, and veterans. They allow us to live our lives.

In the previous chapter, we learned how to change an alpha's mind with BRACE. Now we're going to learn how to make DEALS with alphas when stakes are high and they're even more likely to get triggered.

Make DEALS When Stakes Are High

Talking with Jonny wasn't the first time I had made the connection between influencing alphas and defusing bombs. Several years ago, one of my clients adopted a strength-based coaching initiative. Although I have a background in sport psychology, executive coaching, and counseling psychology, one of my clients adopted a strength-based coaching initiative and requested that all their coaches, including me, get trained. As someone who is always challenging others to grow, it was a good opportunity to challenge myself.

As part of the training, we took a strength-based assessment and were provided a coach to debrief our profile. After a good amount of conversation about the types of executives and surgeons I advise, the coach said, "You enjoy and are good at defusing bombs." I had never thought about my work that way, but there certainly was truth in her insight. I often find myself in engagements where the stakes are high, the client is an alpha, and a turnaround is needed.

For more than two decades I've had the opportunity to do my best to influence strong personalities, and I've learned there are common missteps as well as a recipe for success. As mentioned in the previous chapter, when it comes to dealing with alpha personalities, the most common mistake is to take things personally, which leads to a reactive approach and either taking the person head-on (dominant strength style) or disengaging (submissive strength style). Both of those strategies end poorly, especially when alphas are already tense and more likely to engage in bullying behavior.

Two things need to happen to successfully influence dominant personalities in high-stakes situations. First, you need to move from being reactive to being intentional. Second, you need to change the expected patterns of interaction and treat the bully in a way they haven't been treated before.

To explain how to use both of these strategies, I use the acronym DEALS. DEALS stands for *depersonalize, empathize, align, look for the hook,* and *show Subtle Strength.*

Just as when you need to make a critical decision in any area of your life, following a process helps you remove the emotion and focus on the goal.

The DEALS process is not just about "dealing with" bullies but taking intentional action to make a *deal* with the bully so you can positively influence them. Specifically, it helps you shift from being reactive to being intentional, returns full access to all areas of your Value-Based Power, and makes it less likely you'll get pulled in a direction you don't want to go. Realizing you have the capability to respond rather than react sets you up for success.

Depersonalize

Depersonalize is equally the most challenging and the most critical step. Just as in BRACE, the first and most important step is to shift from reactive to intentional. We don't want them to set the direction, nor do we want their dysfunction to become our dysfunction. To do that, depersonalize the situation: Realize the alpha's reactions have nothing to do with you. Shift your focus from the instinct to make it personal to your intention to win in the long term. This is where your ego agility comes into play.

Empathize

Once you have defused *your* reactivity, you can help defuse the alpha's reactivity by doing something that rarely happens. As crazy as it sounds, *empathize* with the alpha, even if they are acting like a bully. Try to understand why they are behaving this way. If they are making you feel the way you do, it's likely they have very few, if any, real relationships because most people tend to avoid or attack them. You may recall the example of one executive who had been trained to bring a sword and a shield into every conversation—and to use the sword first.

Now that you know more about how our brain works when stressed, you may find it easier to empathize with the alpha. They are likely in a reactive state, just like all of us are from time to time. And if they're in a reactive state, they are also likely to be less strategic, less focused on innovation and collaboration, and stuck in a win/lose mindset.

Neurologically, by empathizing with the alpha, what we are trying to do is to decrease their threat response so they have greater access to their best qualities and are more open to influence. In other words, we are choosing the tend-and-befriend stress response. Remember, you can be in a high-stress situation and not necessarily be reactive. As we learned from the work of Richard Boyatzis, Kelly McGonigal, and Daniel Friedland, showing empathy through positive interactions, like conversations, listening, eye contact, and laughing, can release oxytocin, a hormone that can enhance social bonds in certain situations.

Align

Next, *align* with them. You may recall that *align* is one of the five facets of BRACE found to change someone's mind in our research. Pay them a small compliment; let them know you understand their ambitions. Agree with them to disarm them.

Look for the Hook

Then, *look for the hook*. In every conversation, even the toughest ones, there are opportunities and openings. You may notice certain "coins" that reveal their Motivational Currency, or they may directly mention something meaningful to them. You may notice a pause in the conversation, or they may say something that gives you an advantage. Look for instances where you can connect with what is important to them in order to move forward.

Show Subtle Strength

Finally, *show Subtle Strength*. Alphas often test people by pushing them, and they expect people to either push back harder or completely avoid them. Do neither. Communicate that you aren't a pushover by respectfully and consistently demonstrating your confidence.

Here is a reference chart that summarizes how to make DEALS with alphas.

Step	Key Points	Actions
Depersonalize	A bully's behavior is not about you. Don't take it personally as most people do. Depersonalizing the situation gives you an advantage and more options to influence.	Remind yourself that the bully is behaving this way because of their unmet needs, insecurities, thinking errors, or damaged past.
Empathize	No one feels for someone who is pushing others around. This is why empathy is so powerful. Change the pattern to influence the outcome.	Genuinely try and understand the bully's perspective and their story. Challenge yourself to have empathy for the bully.

Align	Communicate you understand their ambitions. Agree and compliment to lower tension and increase comfort.	Say: "I can see how important X is to you." "Understandably, there is a lot of passion around this topic." "Thank you for putting so much thought into this." "I agree that X is really important."
Look for the hook	Look for the opening or opportunity. Sometimes the hook is when they reveal their primary motivator. Be patient and find the opportunity to agree and move forward.	Ask yourself: What is the bully's primary motivator? What is most important to the bully?
Show Subtle Strength	Always show some type of strength that demonstrates respect and backbone.	Say: "I'm with you on what you want to accomplish. You clearly have a lot of experience in this area. What if we considered a slight adjustment that may increase the chances of achieving what you want?"

During the peak of the COVID-19 crisis, I was fortunate to meet Steve Forti, chief resilience and wellness officer at the Hospital for Special Surgery in New York City. Steve's story is remarkable and featured in the book *The Twenty-Year War*. Steve is a retired Green Beret, among the elite of the special forces.

What I instantly admired about Steve is his straight talk balanced with a raw care for others. His confidence is clear, but he also knows a more subtle approach can be effective when influencing strong personalities. I asked Steve to talk with me about his view on how to influence the toughest people in the toughest times. During my conversation with Steve, I asked a series of questions to get his perspective. Although I hadn't shared the DEALS approach with him, it was remarkable how closely his philosophy and approach aligned with it and offer additional insights into why this approach can be so effective.

Steve believes that bullying is a battle of individual confidence and will. While Steve is a self-aware and socially aware person who cares for others, he advocates taking ownership of your own power and exploring what the person being bullied is contributing to the situation. While no one wants to blame victims of bullying, it is worthwhile to ask, "Am I unintentionally giving this person permission to treat me this way?"

Making DEALS with Alphas: Principles for Success

- Realize it is okay to "lose" in the moment.
- Treat the bully in a way they don't expect.
- Communicate with calm confidence.
- Agree with them and pay them compliments.
- Keep emotion low and intention high.
- Protect yourself from getting pulled into the bully bubble and fighting with the bully on their turf using their rules.

Steve also talked about not taking the situation personally with an acronym someone shared with him. It is EGO: Easily Gets Offended. Our ego is easily offended, and the acronym is a helpful reminder to build our ego agility and not get triggered by interactions that may challenge our status or tap into our insecurities.

He acknowledged the importance of empathizing with the dominant person. We know the strategy of having empathy for a bully is unpopular, but it works because it's genuine, it takes us out of our own emotional experience, and it shifts the cycle and behavioral pattern. To help us empathize more easily, Steve offered the strategy of asking ourselves questions that take the sting out of the bullying, such as, "What is going on in their world that led them to behaving this way?" Much like forgiveness, you are not empathizing with them solely for their benefit; it is beneficial to you as well. In this case, it shifts a potentially emotional reaction to an intentional response.

Above all, Steve suggests remembering you have options. You don't always have to take someone head-on; you can also build alliances with others. We'll explore why and how to build alliances in chapter 10.

What If the Bomb Goes Off?

As we learned from EOD team leader Jonny Walker, the more prepared we are, the less likely it is for a bomb to go off. But when interacting with alphas, even if we prepare as much as possible and put ourselves in the best position possible, there will be times when the bomb goes off and the alpha has an outburst.

If the bomb goes off, it is critical that you stay true to Subtle Strength.

Hit the pause button. Return to the depersonalization process. Remember, this person's reaction isn't about you.

Resist the bully bubble. When an alpha is triggered, they are also very good at triggering others. They can create what feels like a "bully bubble," where you get trapped in their reality and isolated from others. You feel stuck, you feel embarrassed, and you're convinced everyone's looking at you. Before you know it, it seems you have no choice but to do what the bully wants or to end the situation by any means necessary.

Submission (avoidance) or dominance (attack mode) opens the door to the bully bubble. Once you are in it's tough to get out, so don't go in. Remind yourself that the bully is behaving this way because of their unmet needs, insecurities, thinking errors, or damaged past. This in no way excuses the behavior, but your awareness can prevent you from getting pulled into the bully's bubble.

Focus on the big picture of what you want. Is challenging the bully worth it? You may decide it's not worth it, and your best choice is to walk away. If it is worth it, focus on communicating with calm confidence that demonstrates both respect and backbone.

BullyProof Strategy #6: Defuse the Bomb

When an alpha has become a bully, make DEALS with them:

1. *Depersonalize* to shift from reactive to intentional.
2. *Empathize* to connect with the bully's situation and do something
3. they might not expect.
4. *Align* to reflect understanding of their position to lower tension and increase comfort.
5. *Look for the hook* to find the opportunity to agree and move forward.
6. *Show Subtle Strength* to demonstrate respect and backbone.

Because we all enter into a reactive state from time to time, we all have the potential to exhibit bullying behaviors. So what do we do if *we* are the bully?

Awareness, Application, and Alliances

What insights did I have in this chapter?

What will I apply and when?

With whom will I share what I learned?

CHAPTER 7

Wait–Am I a Bully?

One day my wife and I were discussing whether or not I was an alpha. She asked, "Have you ever been in a situation where you wouldn't take charge?" In that moment, I realized I had more alpha than I knew.

In further conversation, she gave me examples of how I can be overly direct and not realize my impact. An example is when I plan work travel. She shared that when I plan work travel, I let her know when I will be away and presume it's okay and she will adjust. I learned when my wife plans travel, it's a multiple-step process that includes ensuring the family and her work is covered, and it ends with her asking me if the dates will work rather than telling me. Contrast this approach with me just telling her the dates I will be gone. My intention was to check something off my to-do list and get the trip booked.

I realized that not only did I have a gender bias, I also engaged in bullying behavior by telling rather than asking and unintentionally prioritizing my time over hers. Now, I try to ask more than I tell and be more mindful of my biases. I will say I am a long way from a success story, but I have made changes that decrease my bullying behaviors, which increases my demonstration of respect for my wife and her time.

I often reflect on where else I may behave this way in my work engagements and friendships. As I mentioned, I grew up in northern New Jersey, just outside New York City, and debate and direct conversations are simply how we communicate. While this may be true, being aware and adapting are critical to our collective success.

What Is a Bully?

There are countless definitions of the word *bully*. For the purposes of this book, we define a bully as someone who consistently gets what they want regardless of the costs. On one hand, we have the extreme examples mentioned in the introduction, such as the Unabomber or people who become involved in mass shootings. But bullying does not always have malicious intent or do major damage.

Bully is a loaded word. Once someone is branded as a bully, it is tough to change those perceptions. How do you determine if someone is a bully? Is there a set of objective behaviors associated with bullying, or does it depend on the experience of the person on the receiving end? Whether someone is a bully can be tricky to unpack because two people on the receiving end of bullying behavior may have very different experiences. One may feel bullied, while the other may actually feel motivated, challenged, or empathetic.

The truth is the person's objective behaviors *and* the other person's experience help determine what bullying is and when it occurs. In the executive leadership space, you will often here about the gap between *intention* and *impact*. They both matter, but when it comes to leadership, impact matters more.

In our discussion of cognitive biases in chapter 3, we mentioned the fundamental attribution error, which is when we find reasons to excuse our failures but blame others for their failures. We all tend to judge ourselves on intent and others on impact. In fact, we can learn a lot about what we think of ourselves and others when we drive. In most places in the Northeast, people drive fast. They want to get from point A to point B and don't want anyone getting in their way or slowing them down. Think back to a time when someone cut you off. What did you think about that person? Those negative thoughts could even result in some people, not me, giving them the "Jersey Bird."

What about when you are rushing to an important meeting and realize you need to get over to exit, and there is someone to your right? You speed up a bit and move over so you can catch your exit. You think to yourself, "It's okay, they will understand I need to get to a meeting."

Were you thinking about the other person's intention when you were the one being cut off?

Why Do People Become Bullies?

While there can be a host of reasons why people become bullies, there are some common ingredients we often see.

- Insecurity
- Lack of friendships
- Previous experience with being bullied
- Poor family life
- History of being controlled by others early in life
- Experiences interactions as win or lose
- Lack of empathy for others
- Lack of self and social awareness
- Unmet needs

The Bully Barometer

In the driving example, we can see at least three elements at work: our subjective intent (what we intended our impact to be), our subjective impact (how others feel as a result of our behavior), and our behaviors themselves. In addition to the subjective elements of intent and impact, it's also helpful to consider someone's objective behaviors. What do bullies do that causes us to define them as bullies?

Below is a quiz I call the Bully Barometer, which will help you more objectively determine if someone is engaging in bullying behavior.

Please think of a person in your life who could potentially be a bully. With this person in mind, go line by line and put a check mark in Column 1 next to all of the behaviors this person engages in.

Does this person . . .

Column 1		Column 2
	win negotiations?	
	tease other people?	
	dominate others?	
	use their position to get what they want?	
	seem comfortable with conflict?	
	make people feel uneasy?	
	give a point of view whether asked or not?	
	take action before others?	
	persuade others?	
	believe compromising is losing?	

	believe empathy gets in the way of getting results?	
	tell more than asks?	
	use their physical presence to persuade?	
	shut down conversations?	
	intimidate others?	
	choose results over relationships?	
	give unsolicited advice?	
	disagree more than agrees?	
	escalate conflicts?	
	manipulate people?	
	undermine others?	
	not truly listen?	
	prompt people if they don't respond quickly enough?	
	ignore requests from others while continuing to make requests?	
	disrupt other people's work?	
	withhold information from others?	
	cite data to show why someone is wrong?	

This list of behaviors exemplifies common bullying behaviors. Take a moment to add up the number of behaviors you have checked for this person. The more of these behaviors a person demonstrates collectively, the stronger their bullying impact is on the people around them. In other words, bullying behaviors are not simply something you have or you don't; they exist on a continuum.

0–3	4–8	9+
Minimal Bullying Impact	Moderate Bullying Impact	Maximum Bullying Impact

Even if the person had the best possible intention, what's the impact of engaging in these behaviors? The impact can be quite large, as we saw in the introduction. As a reminder, one of the biggest challenges of bullying behaviors is that people spend more energy on how they were treated rather than on actual work itself. One of the key findings in our research was that when someone interacts with a consistently dominant person, they will avoid the person or attack the person. **Both of these** actions lead to poor outcomes for all parties.

If you are committed to becoming **BullyProof**, your response to this next activity is crucial. Please do anything you need to do to activate an open mind and a growth mindset. You can always decide that you completely disagree with my next points, but for a few minutes, I invite you to be as objective and intellectually honest as you can.

Please return to the Bully Barometer. In Column 2, put a check mark next to all of the behaviors _you_ engage in.

What was the result? Did you have more or less than the first person? What did you learn about yourself?

As I am writing this chapter, the book cover is complete, and the book is up for presales. Several people I know well have commented that they need this book to deal with a bully at work. While this is likely true, I also know they also need the book to recognize that they too are engaging in bullying behavior.

While others may not call you a "bully," it's likely that all of us engage in bullying behaviors from time to time. Based on my experience facing my own bullying behaviors, I'm hopeful you will reflect on this possibility for several reasons. First, our intentions are important, but our impact is even more important. We can unintentionally strain relationships, intimidate people, and create situations where people are motivated to work against us.

Second, if we realize we all may unintentionally engage in bullying behavior, we will have more empathy for each other. Keep in mind our goal in becoming BullyProof is to protect ourselves and others from being negatively impacted by bullies and to help bullies realize that if they engage in less bullying behavior, everyone wins. The success pie is large enough for us all. Your success does not need to be someone else's failure.

> What bullying behaviors do you recognize in others?
>
> What bullying behaviors do you recognize in yourself?

For all these reasons, I would like to invite us to shift how we think about bullies. As you have seen, it's often less about fixed character traits and more about behaviors. Unless someone has true narcissism or other mental illness, we can all learn to decrease our bullying behaviors.

Emotional Intelligence in Action

One way we can decrease the unintended negative consequences of our behavior is to leverage the four I's of what I call Emotional Intelligence in Action: insight, influence, intention, and impact.

I first began to research emotional intelligence (EI) at Springfield College's Athletic Counseling program when I was studying the psychology of sport and performance. EI was not yet well known, and there was limited data on how to apply the research to practice. So I decided to focus my thesis there.

While attending the American Psychological Association's conference in San Francisco, I was walking in town and happened to pass someone on the street I recognized: Peter Salovey, the researcher who had coined the term *emotional intelligence*. I instantly spun around and asked if he could spare a minute of his time. He did a lot more than that; not only did he invite me to visit him in his office at Yale and offer invaluable insights for my research, he connected me to numerous others working on similar projects.

Today, Peter Salovey is president of Yale University. I will be forever grateful for his guidance, wisdom, and grace.

Since that summer in San Francisco, EI has come a long way. It has been found to predict success in leaders and athletes, and the business case has been well documented.[36] I have often said that EI doesn't have to be complicated, but it does need to be commonly stated. To bridge theory and practice and help people bully less and collaborate more, I created a framework called Emotional Intelligence in Action.[37]

Emotional Intelligence in Action (EIA) allows you to *leverage insight for intentional influence*. Not only does it decrease the negative consequences of reactive behavior, it directly addresses bullying behavior at the source. While reactions are based on feelings, responses are intentional, strategic, and based on facts. Rather than allowing your reactions to determine your impact, the EIA framework allows you to strategically respond with intentional action.

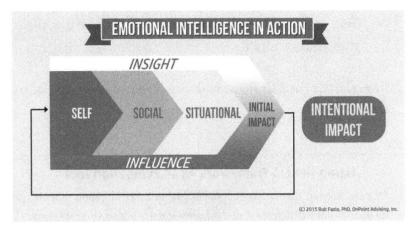

Figure 7.1. Emotional Intelligence in Action

The goal of the EIA framework is *intentional impact*, using the tools of *insight* and *influence* in three areas: *self*, *social*, and *situational*.

- *Self-insight* is the awareness of your thoughts and emotions, and how they influence your actions.
- *Social insight* is the ability to read verbal and nonverbal cues, others' emotions, and your impact on others.
- *Situational insight* is recognizing the power dynamics and politics at work in systems and organizations.
- *Self-influence* is your ability to redirect and motivate yourself.
- *Social influence* is your ability to engage in effective interpersonal interactions.
- *Situational influence* is your ability to initiate positive change in the current setting, culture, business, and/or industry.
- Your *initial impact* is your impact that may or may not match your intention.

- Your *intentional impact* is your desired outcome that aligns with your intention.

You can use the EIA framework either to evaluate a past situation or to plan for a tough future situation.

Using the EIA Framework As an Evaluation Tool

As a tool to evaluate your intentional impact in a past situation, you can move through each element of the framework by asking yourself these questions:

- What was my intended impact?
- What impact did I have?
- How did I do with self-insight: Was I aware of my thoughts and emotions, and how they influenced my actions?
- How did I do with social insight: Was I able to read verbal and nonverbal cues, others' emotions, and my impact on others?
- How did I do with situational insight: Did I recognize the power dynamics and politics at work in the larger system or organization?
- How did I do with self-influence: Was I able to redirect and motivate myself when needed?
- How did I do with social influence: Was I able to engage in effective interpersonal interactions?
- How did I do with situational influence: Was I able to initiate positive change in my current setting, culture, business, and/or industry?
- Knowing what I know now, how can I achieve my intended impact?

> ## Using the EIA Framework As a Planning Tool
>
> As a proactive tool for your next tough situation, you can ask yourself the following questions to prepare to achieve your intentional impact.
>
> - What is my intended impact?
> - Self-insight: Remember to be aware of my thoughts and emotions and how they influence my actions.
> - Social insight: Remember to read verbal and nonverbal cues, others' emotions, and my impact on others.
> - Situational insight: Remember to recognize the power dynamics and politics at work in the larger systems/organization.
> - Self-influence: How can I proactively prepare to redirect and motivate myself when needed?
> - Social influence: How can I proactively prepare to engage in effective interpersonal interactions and strengthen relationships?
> - Situational influence: How can I proactively prepare to initiate positive change in my current setting, culture, business, and/or industry?
> - What else I can do to proactively prepare to achieve my intended impact?

The EIA framework also works as a cycle and ongoing process. The more you use it, the closer your initial impact will be to your intentional impact, the more effective you will be at responding rather than reacting, and the fewer bullying behaviors you will exhibit.

Let's make this framework come to life with an example. I was working with a software engineer, Kyle, who was brilliant. The challenge was that his communication approach and interpersonal skills were getting in the way of his brilliance. I remember our first meeting, and while he was a nice person, I was having a hard time connecting with him. For every example I gave or suggestion I made, he immediately gave a rebuttal based on his experience and the data he thought was important to cite. I realized I needed to take a step back and shift our pattern of interaction.

I said, "Kyle, it's clear to me you are smarter than I am. You know technology and your business more than I ever will. I think I can help you have more influence and get your points of view across more frequently. Would you like to give it a try?" That moment shifted our dynamic from me trying to be right and change him to me trying to help him be right and more successful.

I then had an opening to introduce the idea of EIA. Kyle had very low self-insight and social insight. When insight is low, it is very difficult to match intention with impact. We identified what his intention was, which was to provide the organization with the most accurate information to help them deliver on innovative products. The impact he was having was shutting people down and rubbing them the wrong way because he was coming across as someone who always needed to be the smartest person in the room. We focused on raising his insight about why he communicates in a manner where he challenges everyone publicly and talks over people. He explained that he felt his job was to be the subject-matter expert, and the way people felt during interactions was meaningless.

It took some time, but before meetings and presentations, Kyle started to use the EIA framework as a way to identify his intention and the insights he needed in order to influence in an effective manner. He began to recognize the value of asking questions, not always having to be right, and seeking input from others. As a result, people listened to more of what Kyle had to say and were less distracted by his communication style.

Take Ownership of Your Triggers

One strategy for increasing your EIA self-awareness and self-influence is to become more aware of *emotional hijacks*.

Most of us live under nearly constant pressure, especially time pressure. Combine that pressure with the reactive world we live in, and we have a recipe for action without intention. This tendency gets reinforced as businesses put a premium on a bias for action rather than a bias for strategy. The result is a culture of firefighting, where people often prefer the "fast answer" rather than the right answer.

I'm all about moving forward fast, but not every time and not at the expense of strategy. This bias for action and hyper focus on getting results can increase our chances of engaging in bullying behavior. It's quite easy to rationalize emotional behavior when your intention is getting results. The challenge is the unintended long-term consequences.

Emotional hijacks happen to all of us; when something triggers us, we "lose it" and behave in a reactive manner, as we discussed in chapter 3. When we're in a reactive state, we often feel out of control, which can result in bullying behavior. If we regularly allow our emotional reactions to dominate our behavior, not only will others likely view us as a bully, they'll likely lose respect for us over time. Fortunately, there are some things we can do to minimize the negative consequences of an emotional hijack.

Know Your Emotional Triggers

Your emotional triggers are the people, events, words, and situations that have a strong emotional charge for you. We all have them, and they can be different for everyone. For example, one of my emotional triggers is seeing someone in power take advantage of someone else or manipulate a situation to their advantage. Yours may be when someone is repeatedly late for meetings, or doesn't clean up after themselves, or interrupts you when you're talking. Whatever your emotional triggers are, if you aren't aware of them, they're more likely to take over your behavior.

Respect Your Triggers

Our thoughts are part of who we are and our experience. Our thoughts and perceptions are often what lead to our triggers, whether we realize it or not. We do not have the power to stop our thinking, but we do have the power to control our responses.

Many strategies focus on trying to push our thoughts away—for example, the more we dislike the thought, the more we should try to push it away. It's almost as if we are bullying our thoughts, which is only going to make them come back stronger. Remember, our brain can be a bully. We now know that dominance doesn't work with bullying behavior; a better approach is respect. We can respect our brain's thoughts by allowing them to come and go. They don't have power unless we give them power.

Getting triggered is part of life. If we respect our triggers and realize there will be situations where we are likely to get triggered, they will have less of an impact on us.

Have a Strategy Ready to Defuse the Power of the Emotion

You may not be able to stop the emotion, but you don't have to fan it into flame either. Do something to maintain your composure in the moment, whether it's leaving the room temporarily or saying to yourself, "This emotion will pass, and when it does, I will decide what to do."

What are your triggers?

What strategy can you use to keep them from triggering a reactive state?

Everyone experiences emotional hijacks differently. Some people are easily able to manage them, while others experience high intensity and have great difficulty keeping their composure. Either way, there's no need to be blindsided by emotion. Whether your emotional hijacks are minor or intense, the more aware you are of your emotional triggers, the more quickly you will recognize an emotional hijack when it happens and the more strategic you will become in managing it.

Build More, Bully Less

The opposite of bullying behaviors are behaviors that build up ourselves and others. Our Value-Based Power framework provides a strong guide for our motivations and actions—and also for the building behaviors that support the values, ambitions, and challenges of yourself, others, your organization, and society as a whole.

		Was I aware?	Did I take action?
Self	Values		
	Ambitions		
	Challenges		
Others	Values		
	Ambitions		
	Challenges		
Organization	Values		
	Ambitions		
	Challenges		

Society	Values		
	Ambitions		
	Challenges		

Figure 7.2. Value-Based Power Worksheet

Just like the EIA framework, and as you learned in chapter 1, you can use the Value-Based Power framework to evaluate past situations or to plan for future situations.

To use the Value-Based Power framework as a "report card" for building behaviors in a past situation, ask yourself these questions:

- Was I aware of my values, ambitions, and challenges, and did I take action accordingly?
- Was I aware of the values, ambitions, and challenges of others, and did I take action accordingly?
- Was I aware of the values, ambitions, and challenges of the organization, and did I take action accordingly?
- Was I aware of the values, ambitions, and challenges of society, and did I take action accordingly?

To use the Value-Based Power framework to plan for building behaviors in an upcoming situation, ask yourself these questions:

- What are my values, ambitions, and challenges, and how will I take action to support them in this situation?
- What are the values, ambitions, and challenges of others, and how will I take action to support them in this situation?
- What are the values, ambitions, and challenges of the organization, and how will I take action to support them in this situation?
- What are the values, ambitions, and challenges of society, and how will I take action to support them in this situation?

Remember, if you'd like to download an editable version of this Value-Based Power worksheet, go to OnPointAdvising.com/BullyProof.

If we all start with ourselves and make a commitment to bully less and build more, we will create more collaboration and results.

BullyProof Strategy #7: Minimize Bullying Behaviors

1. Take the Bully Barometer.
2. Use the Emotional Intelligence in Action framework to decrease bullying behaviors.
3. Use the Value-Based Power framework to increase building behaviors.

In Part 1, we have covered key tools and strategies for becoming BullyProof to support yourself and others. In Part 2, we will now focus on tools and strategies for becoming BullyProof to support your organization and society as a whole.

Awareness, Application, and Alliances

What insights did I have in this chapter?

What will I apply and when?

With whom will I share what I learned?

| Part 2 |

BullyProof Your Organization and Strengthen Society

CHAPTER 8

Growth Leadership in Times of Crisis

Many moments are etched into our minds from when we first heard about the COVID-19 pandemic. I was in Santa Clara for a client meeting and could feel the concern building. Travel was getting more difficult, and I was happy to get home without any challenges. One of my strongest memories was seeing Mark Cuban, the owner of the Dallas Mavericks, stand up at the start of a game to let the referees know the game had been cancelled due to COVID-19. From that moment on, leaders began making decisions that would stay with them and their organizations for the rest of their lives.

Mark Cuban was the first person I saw step up and say he would be paying all of his employees during the crisis. This was before any government aid was available and before we had any clarity about how the pandemic would impact our lives. His leadership demonstrated a people-first approach and the result was loyalty and followership. He took away a major source of fear—financial ruin—for his employees. We all won't be in a place to make huge decisions like this, nor will we all be able to create financial safety for those around us, but we can lead with a people-first approach that leads to growth for ourselves, our people, our organization, and society.

How Crisis Impacts an Organization

The way companies and employees handle a crisis has large financial implications. A 2017 report by Aon found that in the current digital age the impact of reputation events on stocks has doubled. In the aftermath of a crisis, how a company's management prepares, handles, and behaves can add 20 percent of value or lose 30 percent of value.[38] According to the World Health Organization, depression and anxiety, more likely during any crisis, have a significant economic impact. The approximate cost to the global economy is $1 trillion lost in productivity annually.[39] Given the perfect storm of the predictors of anxiety experienced during the COVID-19 crisis, such as lack of control, ambiguity, no clear path, and constant media coverage, that number is likely to be larger.[40]

In times of crisis, we all have a responsibility to take ownership of our power and take care of ourselves, our people, our organizations, and society. Too often I see people who are not in charge just sit back and criticize leaders and organizations rather than trying to be a positive influence. If you are in a position of power, prepare now to lead well in a crisis. If you are not in a position of power, you can influence leaders so they can effectively lead. Think of strengthening your crisis leadership skills as buying insurance. No one enjoys paying for insurance, but they love that they did when there is an accident. Master Whitaker, founder of Urban Defense in Philadelphia, when talking about self-defense, reminds people, "It is better to have it and not need it than to need it and not have it." His philosophy stands true for crisis leadership as well.

Tragic Optimism and Post-Traumatic Growth

The best leaders during crisis don't just get through the event; they find a way for the crisis to be a catalyst for growth. In Viktor Frankl's life-changing book *Man's Search for Meaning*, he talked about the importance of *tragic optimism*.

> Let us first ask ourselves what should be understood by "a tragic optimism." In brief it means that one is, and remains, optimistic in spite of the "tragic triad," . . . a triad which consists of . . . (1) pain; (2) guilt; and (3) death.
>
> This . . . raises the question, How is it possible to say yes to life in spite of all that? How . . . can life retain its potential meaning in spite of its tragic aspects? After all, "saying yes to life in spite of everything," . . . presupposes that life is potentially meaningful under any conditions, even those which are most miserable. And this in turn presupposes the human capacity to creatively turn life's negative aspects into something positive or constructive.
>
> In other words, what matters is to make the best of any given situation. . . . hence the reason I speak of a tragic optimism . . . an optimism in the face of tragedy and in view of the human potential which at its best always allows for: (1) turning suffering into a human achievement and accomplishment; (2) deriving from guilt the opportunity to change oneself for the better; and (3) deriving from life's transitoriness an incentive to take responsible action.[41]

Frankl's work was based on his experience during the Holocaust, one of the most terrible events in history. Even here he concluded that it was possible to turn suffering into achievement, guilt into personal growth, and lack of meaning into responsible action.

The research of Richard Tedeschi and Lawrence Calhoun, founders of Post-Traumatic Growth, supports the idea that post-traumatic growth is possible. Factors that correlate with growth after crisis include emotional social support, higher levels of perceived threat and/or harm, extraversion, openness to experience, agreeableness, conscientiousness, self-efficacy, problem-focused coping, and positive reinterpretation.[42] Although some of these factors may be innate to the person or the event, most can be learned.

Alphas and Crisis Leadership

I have had the opportunity to lead and advise people during some of the toughest times in recent history. These include working with hospitals during the peak of the COVID-19 crisis, September 11, the Virginia Tech shooting, Hurricane Katrina, and countless other crises. I say "opportunity" because these were times when stakes were high and emotions were even higher. If people let you in during these times, it's a privilege to be able to learn, support, and guide them to create outcomes that are as positive as possible.

Based on these experiences, I have learned that leaders can do a lot of damage or a lot of good, depending on their approach. For example, alphas are critical to success before, during, and after a crisis. They are the people willing to take the lead despite not having clarity. Yet their level of comfort in setting direction and making decisions can be helpful or hurtful during a crisis. If someone is an unaware nonadaptive alpha, they can do great damage to an organization. The reason is that in times of pressure and high stress, people double down on what is most comfortable to them and their natural strengths. I call this "the crease." Think of a piece of paper folded down the middle, where the fold is now a crease. Let's say you want the paper to lie flat and not have a fold in it. It would take intentional work to "decrease the crease" so that the paper would not tend to move along the fold. We all have "creases," and it's important that as pressure goes up, we all learn how to hit the pause button so we don't just behave based on autopilot.

Whether you are an alpha who is leading through a crisis or interacting with an alpha who is in charge, the practices of Growth Leadership will increase your chances of creating positive outcomes.

Growth Leadership in Times of Crisis

Approximately twenty years ago, the OnPoint Advising team created a process called Growth Consulting to support people's growth following loss and crisis. This approach was designed to meet people where they were and to influence people toward positive outcomes in some of the most negative times.

Similarly, a Growth Leadership approach focuses on helping you, your team, your organization, and society grow through crisis and adversity. To be the best possible leader in the worst of times, you need first to be able to strengthen yourself so you can strengthen and connect with others.

During a crisis, many mistakes are made because pressure is coming from many different areas. As you may have already guessed, the Value-Based Power framework is a helpful resource for knowing where to invest your time and effort during a crisis to maximize the growth of everyone involved.

Following the Value-Based Power framework, there are four core areas to focus on during a crisis: self-leadership, team leadership, organizational leadership, and social leadership. All of them are important, and failing to pay attention to one can have a negative impact on others. For example, if a leader focuses solely on getting business results and doesn't demonstrate their understanding of the crisis's impact on team members, employees can become disengaged or burnt out.

Think of the leaders you observed as they navigated the COVID-19 crisis.
- Which leaders seemed to have a balanced focus?
- Which seemed to do what came first and naturally to them?
- Which approach had better outcomes for everyone involved?

Figure 8.1. Using Value-Based Power during a Crisis

Self-Leadership

Self-leadership includes managing and communicating your brand and taking care of yourself (i.e., managing your stress). The more effectively you are able to lead yourself, the stronger the platform you will create for leading others. Everything will seem out of balance during times of crisis, and that is because most things *are* out of balance. It is your job to find a way to maintain some type of personal homeostasis to keep yourself grounded and allow you to make strong, strategic decisions that will help your organization grow.

Ensuring you have a strong sense of your strengths, weaknesses, and derailers is essential, especially in times of uncertainty and crisis. As a leader, people will be looking to you for answers, so you need to minimize your blind spots and maximize the positive impact you have on others. You are the most direct link to the organizational atmosphere. The healthier, more energizing, and more engaging you are, the more motivated people will be to meet the challenges of the crisis and grow through the experience.

Based on our research and experience, we have identified eleven factors found to predict growth through adversity and overall well-being. To discover where your strengths and growth areas lie in the area of Growth Leadership, you can take a no-cost Growth Through Adversity Survey (GTAS) at HoldtheDoor.com. Andy High at Penn State University recently volunteered his time to validate the GTAS and help us focus on what is most helpful for people to focus on.

Team Leadership

Your ability to understand the experience of your direct reports and peers, as well as rally their support, will be crucial. Focus on taking care of your team as they take care of the crisis. Be sure the messages your team receives and sends are consistent with your messages and are aligned with the organization's overall crisis growth strategy.

Organizational Leadership

Practical results in a crisis are more important than you might think. Establishing safety and taking care of people financially are core components of handling a crisis well. If the organization fails, it will cause an avalanche of additional crises. It may seem contradictory to say to focus on the organization and to focus on people. They actually can go hand in hand if you think through the proper strategy and the implication of each step along the way. Growing the organization may not happen within a short time frame, and that is precisely why early decisions need to be informed by a long-term, strategic perspective.

Social Leadership

If we can focus beyond ourselves and work, a crisis can also provide a powerful opportunity to strengthen society. Whether you care about making an impact on society or not, people will be watching how socially responsible you are in a time of crisis. How leaders handle crises translates into how outsiders permanently view the leader and the organization. Therefore, it is absolutely critical to take steps to connect with people outside the organization. Depending on the crisis, those people may include family members of those affected by the crisis, media contacts, investors, and other key stakeholders.

What to Do during a Crisis

Now that you're familiar with the concept of Growth Leadership and how to balance your focus with Value-Based Power, let's take a look at what needs to happen during a crisis from a Growth Leadership perspective.

I use the acronym SPEAKERS: *safety, people first, emotional intelligence, articulate your vision, knowledge, evaluate, reach out,* and *sacrifice.*

Safety

Ensure that you do everything you can to restore safety and stabilize the situation. If the crisis includes physical or emotional danger, you want to demonstrate immediately that you are taking all steps necessary to keep people out of harm's way.

People First

People are your most important resource, and you want to demonstrate that you care about them. Crises require high physical and emotional presence from leaders. People need to see you as often as possible and as empathetic as possible. At the same time, it's important that people are being informed and being heard.

Emotional Intelligence (EI)

In times of high pressure and extreme change, feelings can be overwhelming. Your awareness of your emotional responses, your ability to integrate thoughts and feelings, and your ability to communicate appropriately are crucial. You also need to be able to accurately anticipate and read the emotional reactions of those around you affected by the crisis.

Articulate Your Vision

Clarity rules. Your message needs to be clear and instill confidence in those around you. Connect people to the future of the business. Find the balance between acting to stabilize the crisis in the present and demonstrating your passion for the future. Display leadership behaviors consistent with your vision and emphasize you are doing everything you can to ensure stability and growth in the future. *You want to communicate early and often.*

Knowledge

In times of crisis, people look to leaders for information and expect them to communicate that information. Become an expert in crisis communication and instilling confidence based on facts.

Evaluate

Get feedback on how you are doing. Seek input from people affected by the crisis. It is alright to get feedback and decide you need to change things, stay the same, or seek more feedback. It is not alright to fail to see how effective or ineffective you are as a leader.

Reach Out

Consult with as many experts as your time and resources will allow. Gaining different perspectives from a variety of sources will assist you in decision-making and ensure diversity of thought. You have a certain expertise; during a crisis rely on experts around you whom you can trust. Examples of people to reach out to are media contacts, lawyers, counselors, and people who are directly affected. The "go it alone" attitude that may have worked in the past will not serve you well in a crisis. It is a time to pool resources and consult experts.

Sacrifice

In times of crisis, people need to know you are able and willing to make adjustments for the long-term greater good. You may need to give more to employees than you typically would or personally sacrifice something to show you care and realize this is a collective effort.

Five Keys for Implementing Growth Leadership

Now that we know what to do, let's look at how to do it. The image below provides an overview of the five keys to implement Growth Leadership in times of crisis. Like many of the frameworks you have learned in this book, it can be used as both a planning template and a checklist to ensure you are spending time on the correct communication and influence strategies. Each of the five areas have calibration questions to get you focused in the right direction.

5 Keys for
Growth Leadership in Times of Crisis

1. START WITH SELF TO HELP OTHERS

Energizers
Drainers
Triggers
Emotional Intelligence
Stress Management
Enjoyment & Passion

*How am I strengthening
and preparing
myself to lead?
What am I likely to do
right and wrong?*

2. SEE THE SITUATION

State of the Business
  Now & Long Term
Impact on People
Control vs. Can't Control

*What can I control;
what can I not?
What do people
need now?
What does the
business need now?*

3. COMMUNICATE WITH A SELECTIVE STYLE

Visionary
Business Focused
Purposeful
Collaborative
Relational
Calm Confidence

*Which style comes
naturally, and which
do I need to develop or
ask someone to
communicate for me?*

4. TAILOR TO ALL MOTIVATIONAL CURRENCIES®
BUT START WITH PEOPLE

People
Performance
Power
Purpose

*How can I lead by
focusing on people first
and tap into what
matters most?*

5. GO FOR GROWTH

New Opportunities
  for People & the
  Business
Learning
Future Focus

*What is the future-
focused growth story
of employees and the
business?*

Figure 8.2. Five Keys for Growth Leadership in Times of Crisis

Mistakes Often Made by Leaders during a Crisis

Even when you're intentionally following these frameworks, mistakes can happen—especially when pressure is high and timing is critical. Here are a few of the most common ones.

Listening Only to Those Who Agree with You

It is dangerous to only create solutions or navigate a crisis with people who always agree with you. Intentionally stack your crisis team with people who are credible and courageous enough to disagree with you on substantial issues. If you are always agreeing, you aren't seeing the full picture.

The Way You Handle the Crisis Becomes the Crisis

This one is common because most people aren't prepared (see Four Things to Get Right below). Businesses have a way of trying to push back or cover things up, and that pours fuel on the fire. Be honest and transparent and take the medicine of any mistakes or missteps. People will always find a way to uncover what was covered up.

Failing to Prepare for the Next Crisis

A failure to prepare for the next crisis sets you up to be blindsided. We have an optimism bias in the United States. We are conditioned to believe that everything will be OK. While that may feel good, the truth is the next crisis or uncertain time is around the corner. Take time to think through what could happen to impact the business and what you will do. It doesn't mean walking around saying the sky is falling. It's means being proactive and strategic to create a more positive outcome.

Growth Leadership Principles for Times of Crisis

- Lead yourself as you prepare to lead others.
- Manage yourself before you manage the crisis.
- Focus on people first.
- Leverage Value-Based Power for balanced influence.
- Be proactive rather than reactive.
- Respond rather than react.
- Build your people's confidence so they can do what needs to be done, and hold people accountable after the crisis has been stabilized.
- Be fact based, not fear based.
- Demonstrate a calm confidence.
- Anything you communicate externally you need to communicate internally.
- Your behavior will define your brand and the organization's perceived values.
- Feel slow, think fast.
- Remember the first decision is not always the best decision.
- Ensure that handling the crisis does not become the crisis.

Four Steps to Get Right

Although everyone makes mistakes, some mistakes cost more than others. Here are the four most important things to get right during a crisis.

Sacrifice and Show Up

In March 2020, Lou Shapiro, CEO of the Hospital for Special Surgery in New York City, reallocated 85 percent of its resources to be on the front lines to battle COVID-19.[43] This decision was not easy because it put some of our country's elite surgeons and healthcare professionals right on the front lines in an uncertain time when the science and data were not yet clear. In short, he sacrificed elective surgeries for the greater good.

Just before the peak of the pandemic in New York, Mr. Shapiro said, "First thing is, 'What are your values and principles?' Second thing is, 'What decisions do you make against them?' It has nothing to do with money. It has to do with winning this war. This war is against COVID-19. Period. End of discussion. All hands on deck. No one is excused from participating to fight this battle."[44]

His courage to sacrifice revenue and "show up" by leading with a people-first approach and laser focus on safety helped New York and the country as a whole get through a devastating crisis.

Don't Hit the Easy Button; Explore Your Options

In turbulent times, people want relief—which often causes executives to go with the first solution instead of taking the time to explore further options. As we discussed earlier, a common mistake is to listen only to people who agree with you. Be sure to have a diverse range of people around you willing to disagree to widen your options before a decision is made. People confuse the importance of *communicating* early with *making a decision* too early.

That common mistake often leads to another we mentioned above: the way you handle the crisis can become the crisis. For example, when an incident with a treadmill resulted in a child's death, Peloton initially relied on logic to defend their treadmills' overall safety. Rather than using the SPEAKERS approach, they brought data to a war that was going to be fought with emotion, and that became the story.

There Is Such a Thing As Bad PR. Get Good at It.

Perhaps if you are a movie star looking to build Instagram followers, the lame advice "no PR is bad PR" might work for you but not when it comes to business. A company can work decades to build up a brand, and one comment from the CEO can take it away in a minute. Think back to BP CEO Tony Hayward during the handling of the Gulf of Mexico oil spill. This is the quote he will always be remembered by: "I want my life back." Not the best look when eleven people lost their lives. He and BP became even more of a villain. Again, the handling of the crisis became the crisis.

Any executive who doesn't actively train themselves and their company's spokespeople in media relations does a disservice to the business, shareholders, and employees. Reporters are trained to make headlines, and they love the "gotcha" moment. Having expertise in emotional resourcefulness, presenting under pressure, and engaging in an interview where you are not in favor is critical.

Lack of clarity, control, and capability create the perfect storm for anxiety, burnout, and disengagement. Americans are attracted to and addicted to confidence. But a certain type of confidence works best: calm confidence. Leveraging your Subtle Strength and Value-Based Power will serve you very well. Calm confidence that demonstrates respect and backbone and is fact based gives you the best chance of meeting people where they are and leading them to where they need to go. This style of communication increases the chance you can provide hope and a plan for the people who need it most and create a bond of trust. It builds confidence and creates followership. Mastering interpersonal effectiveness in conversations and presentations allows for your messages to be heard.

Expect the Next Crisis and Prepare

According to PwC, 20 percent of companies say COVID-19 actually had a positive impact on their organization, and they attribute much of it to organizational resilience.[45] Turbulent times will continue to happen. As we learned earlier, research has identified key factors for post-traumatic growth. Why not be proactive and build your Growth Leadership skills prior to the next event? You and your organization will become more able to not only remain resilient but lead others through the event. Even if you're not experiencing a crisis, the Growth Leadership approach will help you achieve your goals in any situation.

BullyProof Strategy #8: Practice Growth Leadership in Times of Crisis

1. Commit to growing through crisis and helping your organization do the same.
2. Take the GTAS at HoldtheDoor.com to learn about yourself and build your growth skills.
3. Use the Value-Based Power framework to set your focus.
4. Use the SPEAKERS framework to know what to do during a crisis.
5. Use the Five Keys for Growth Leadership to implement it effectively.

The Chinese symbol for crisis contains two characters: the first represents danger and the second opportunity. While crisis always provides an opportunity to grow, growth doesn't just happen. It takes preparation, intention, and a diverse, collaborative approach. The more prepared you are to lead yourself and others through a crisis, the less negative impact it will have.

Awareness, Application, and Alliances

What insights did I have in this chapter?

What will I apply and when?

With whom will I share what I learned?

CHAPTER 9

The Importance of Alpha Women

"I t's just not worth it. I don't want to get caught up in the ego-driven screaming matches." Those are the words of a female senior executive who recently got promoted. I was working with her as her executive advisor, and her identified area of development was to increase her executive presence. Over the past twenty years of working in this field, I have learned that "executive presence" is often code for "act more like a man and push people around." Many organizations create a culture that rewards dysfunctional behavior often rooted in aggressive debate.

This executive—let's call her Trey—was competent, confident, and a strong relationship builder. Here was the irony of her situation: Over her years of interacting with alpha males, she had been branded as "intimidating," while her male counterparts were viewed as "business-first focused." As a result, she learned to become passive and disengage. This cost the organization a great deal.

Rather than morph her into someone who gets into emotional arguments and stops listening, we needed to find a way for her to be perceived as strong without falling into the cycle of dysfunction. We both realized what really needed to change was the culture and what was rewarded within that culture. We wondered, "How many junior people have valuable input to share but just do not give their point of view and are inaccurately perceived as passive or incompetent?"

Advocating for Women Leaders Is Everyone's Responsibility

There are countless stories similar to Trey's where women have learned to be silent instead of embracing their natural leadership abilities.

Although women make up the majority of the population (50.8 percent of the US population) and earn the majority of undergraduate (57 percent) and graduate degrees (59 percent), they are significantly underrepresented in leadership positions.

For example, women are

- 45 percent of legal associates but 22.7 percent of partners and 19 percent of equity partners;[46]
- 40 percent of all physicians and surgeons but 16 percent of permanent medical school deans;[47]
- earners of the majority of doctorates for eight consecutive years but 32 percent of full professors and 30 percent of college presidents;[48]
- 61 percent of accountants and auditors, 53 percent of financial managers, and 37 percent of financial analysts but only 12.5 percent of chief financial officers in Fortune 500 companies;[49] and
- 5 percent of CEO positions in Fortune 500 companies and 7.8 percent of CEO positions in S&P 500 companies.[50]

There are a variety of reasons for this gender leadership gap, but at least one reason is that women are not treated the same as men in the workplace. Perhaps the clearest evidence is in the language we use. According to a Pew Research Center study, 67 percent of respondents viewed the word "powerful" as positive when associated with men, while 92 percent viewed it as negative when associated with women. "Strength" was seen as positive for men but not for women. "Ambition" and "leadership" were viewed as positive for men but negative for women, while "caring" and "compassion" were viewed as positive for women but negative for men.[51]

I've seen this gender bias countless times in my own work with executives and surgeons.

Here are some things my clients or I have heard men say:

"I can hire the man you recommend for your replacement, but I'd have to pay him 20 to 30 percent more."
–Senior executive at a Fortune 100 bank to a woman who just got a promotion

"Why would she do that?"
–Senior executive at a Fortune 100 healthcare company about a woman who was up for a promotion and got pregnant

"We need to hire more men."
–Senior executive in a Fortune 50 company during a tour of a new facility

Women are expected to thrive in a workplace culture where the rules and roles were created by men—and when they are viewed as inherently unable to succeed at those rules and roles.[52] When they do exhibit characteristics that appear strong, powerful, ambitious, or dominant, they are often criticized, demeaned, or branded. When they get frustrated and triggered by these impossible and contradictory expectations, people assume they can't handle the job and their career is at risk.

The natural tendency is to disengage and yield; the cost of speaking up or leading just doesn't seem worth it. But the even greater cost is that they lose their voice and credibility, and the bullying behavior continues.

> At your workplace, are women treated differently than men? If so, how?

As of July 1, 2020, Goldman Sachs announced they won't help companies go public unless they have at least one "diverse" board candidate, with a particular focus on women.[53] They found that companies with a woman on the board perform better than companies that don't have a woman on their board. Similarly, Nasdaq has proposed that all companies listed on the US exchange be required to disclose their board of directors' diversity statistics and most companies be required to have (or explain why they don't have) at least two "diverse" directors, including at least one woman.[54]

These initiatives are a start to closing the gender gap. One way to quickly close the gap is to appreciate and accelerate the rise of alpha women.

Why Alpha Women Should Lead the Way

I realize my experience and perspective comes from being a white male, and with that come my own biases. Everyone has their own experiences and perspectives, but I'd like to share what I believe may be helpful as we all seek to level the playing field for women and men in the workplace.

My intention is not to put more of a burden on women to close the gender gap on their own or to suggest that women in some way need to change. Quite the opposite. Based on my work with organizations, I have seen that alphas—both male and female—are key to paving the way for organizational change and getting people to realize the importance of advocating for women and social change. An example of the value of an alpha is someone who is dedicated to environmental, social, and corporate governance (ESG) and is confident and courageous when rallying people to the business who behave in accordance with those values.

We have defined *alpha* as someone who takes the lead in a situation regardless of whether they are the identified leader or subject-matter expert. Being an alpha is neither bad nor good, and, of course, they can be men or women. Although alpha women have the same basic characteristics as alpha men, they also face the same challenges all women face in the workplace. This means they also have some unique opportunities.

According to our research,
- women are happier with their life than men;
- women have more mentors than men; and
- women perceive other women are easier to have conversations with than men.

Harvard Business Review has estimated that 70 percent of all senior executives are alpha men.[55] This doesn't mean that there are fewer alpha women, it means that men have been given more opportunities at executive levels. What I have learned in my work with executives and surgeons is that men tend to be proud to be an alpha and women tend to apologize for it. For men, being an alpha is often socially accepted. For women, it's slightly more complicated, but it shouldn't be.

Alphas can be strong, positive leaders in any organization. Not all alphas talk over people, argue, or drive objectives at the expense of inclusion or collective wisdom. As a reminder from chapter 2, alphas can fall into one of four categories: the unaware non-adaptive, the unaware adaptive, the aware nonadaptive, and the aware adaptive. The most dangerous alpha is the unaware non-adaptive alpha, who is often seen as a bully. The aware adaptive alphas, whether they are male or female, are the most successful at influencing others because they know when to turn up or turn down their alpha. They also have the ability to buffer the negative impact of unaware nonadaptive alphas, who are often the reason for abusive power and dysfunction.[56]

Some research indicates that alpha women may be more likely to be aware adaptive alphas. We know from the research on emotional intelligence that women tend to engage in more behaviors associated with self-awareness, empathy, and conflict management. According to Richard E. Boyatzis, Daniel Goleman, and Korn Ferry's Emotional and Social Competency Inventory (ESCI),

- women are 86 percent more likely than men to be seen as consistently emotionally self-aware;
- women are 45 percent more likely than men to be seen as consistently empathetic; and
- women outperform men in the competencies of coaching and mentoring, influence, inspirational leadership, con-

flict management, organizational awareness, adaptability, teamwork, and achievement orientation.[57]

Also, according to research on men's and women's communication styles, women are more likely to be collaborative, empathetic, aware of nonverbal cues, and good listeners.[58] These traits increase the probability that an alpha woman is aware and adaptive and can naturally buffer the downside of other types of alphas around them.

Who are the alpha women in your home, workplace, organizations, or community?

Are you an alpha woman?

Gender does not determine whether or not someone is an effective leader; their leadership and interpersonal skills do. However, with an estimated 70 percent of top leadership positions filled by alpha males, we can learn a lot from people who demonstrate behaviors usually associated with a feminine approach to leadership. That's why it's critical that all of us—men and women, alphas and non-alphas—accelerate alpha women's paths into leadership roles with positional power.

I encourage all women to embrace their inner alpha. If women own their inner alpha, they have an opportunity to expand their influence, take on positions that matter to them, and further increase the good they are already doing in the world.

Examples of Alpha Women Leaders Who Have Strengthened Society

Despite the challenges alpha women typically face, we have many positive examples of alpha women leaders who have demonstrated Value-Based Power and strengthened society. Here are a few that stand out to me.

Jacinda Ardern, New Zealand's prime minister, led her country through the initial COVID-19 pandemic with overt and Subtle Strength. Through her frequent communications and Facebook Live videos, she demonstrated clear empathy and offered encouraging suggestions as someone who was experiencing this crisis alongside her citizens. By taking decisive action quickly, New Zealand was able to keep the coronavirus out of the country for over a year. Early in the pandemic, 84 percent of New Zealanders approved of the government's response to the crisis and 88 percent trusted the government to make the right decisions about the pandemic moving forward. Although public approval fell when later variants breached New Zealand's borders, Ardern's ratings remained far higher than her political rivals.[59]

Becky Quick, CNBC anchor, has interviewed some of world's most powerful people, such as Warren Buffett, Charlie Munger, Bill Gates, and Alan Greenspan. In fact, Warren Buffett gives her the exclusive interview during the yearly Berkshire Hathaway shareholder meeting. As a coanchor on CNBC's *Squawk Box*, she sits between two alpha men, Joe Kernen and Andrew Ross Sorkin, facilitating conversations with Subtle Strength, calm confidence, and humor, without getting pulled into their fights.

Becky masterfully disarms some of the most powerful people in the financial world and does it with class, candor, and often a hint of humor. Every morning I watch *Squawk Box* with my girls. Reese, my five-and-a-half-year-old, always asks to put on the "Markets," and I am grateful she can see someone like Becky Quick to model the combination of Subtle Strength and intelligence.

And then there's Cathy Flavin, founder of LeaderMom® and Whole Leader, who has been researching and consulting on leadership for over two decades. Her research focuses on top performing and emerging women. Cathy and I worked together, and we instantly became friends and thought partners. I learn from her and her team constantly, and genuine care for others is always at the top of her list. She has worked with Fortune 500 companies and some of the top financial institutions in the world.

I asked if Cathy could share some of her advice based on her research and work related to women in the workplace and beyond. Here is what she said:

> At this moment in history, our task is to dismantle generations of learned mindsets, behaviors, and biases in systems that were not built by or for many of us. Those unconscious, pernicious, subtext assumptions amount to daily bullying for many of us.
>
> An example is when one female executive, who was stunningly qualified to run an organization, received the following comment from a female board member: "You are exceptional, and your ideas are so compelling, but we were expecting an elder statesman." Translation: "You are an excellent candidate, but you do not compute yet in my well-intended brain." The unconscious wiring that makes our subconscious picture of leadership look like a six-foot-tall, sixty-year-old white guy—that is the invisible bully you, me, our coaches, and all of us need to get better at, and braver about, fighting.

While wiring is deep, the good news we can outsmart it. We need models of leadership that appeal to more of us. So many of the beliefs we have about what leading requires are not consistent with the evidence and tragically limit who leadership appeals to. Because research is showing that motherhood-related biases and penalties are a primary reason we don't have more women in senior and executive leadership, in our LeaderMom™ work we are tapping the wisdom of high performers who are also highly engaged in their families and communities. These "unicorns" offer more sustainable models of leadership that combine being excellent at work and being a committed parent. That research and the collective wisdom of these leaders led us to found Whole Leader for all of us. Make no mistake, gendered assumptions that overassociate women with family and men with career ultimately limit all of us, so we all have to go after them. If you think you have some status to lose, you have way more to gain than you know.

Cathy offers the following advice for leaders:

- Tell the high-performing, high-potential women in your world two things: *you belong* in leadership, and leadership is learnable. And before you list what they don't know yet or gaps they may need to close, make the value they do provide ridiculously clear to you and them.
- Please prepare them to navigate biases but not take them personally or accept them. Not doing so is the equivalent of sending someone into a terrible storm with no raincoat or umbrella.

- There is a great Ted Lasso quote: "Enter the arena, but bring a knife." Please make sure the coaches you hire are savvy about how pernicious bias can be and are able to cut the bias away from the useful insights that help people understand where their value is and how they can grow and scale as leaders.

I have seen Cathy's insights and research make an impact. Her work gives women and men practical ways to see things more accurately and take action.

Own Your Alpha—and Advocate for Other Alpha Women

Once you are committed to advocating for alpha women leaders, how exactly do you do that—especially if that leader is yourself? Consider the following suggestions based on what I have learned from working with successful and influential women executives.[60]

Know Your Organization's Culture

Every organization is unique, as is every organization's culture. Before you leap into action, answer these questions first.

- How is credibility earned?
- What behaviors get people promoted and why?
- What gets people demoted or in trouble?
- How do people gain power and influence?
- What missteps tend to stick?

Your answers will help you decide which strategy will be most effective and when.

Apologize Less

If you disagree or have a different point of view, you can voice that view without apologizing. You can be collaborative and clear at the same time. Many people apologize before they make a point, and it weakens their argument. Rather than apologizing, recognize what is said and then state your view.

Advocate for Initiatives Outside of Gender

I'm not saying don't advocate for women. I am saying have stances and partnerships and get involved in additional movements. Businesses are guilty of expecting women to be the leaders of women advocacy groups, and it can take them away from their work. Take on initiatives in addition to gender equality. This will help people view you as a credible resource and leader, and you won't get branded as someone who only focuses on gender. Men need to do more adapting in this area and not think of women in a narrow-minded way.

Create Alliances with Powerful and Powerless People

We know that relationships are crucial to success. The more you can diversify your relationships to include both powerful and powerless people, the more positive impact you can have. As an alpha, you are naturally an influencer. Use this influence to build alliances with powerful people so you can accomplish what you think is important. In regard to people who do not have positional power, understand what is important to them and advocate for them. Help them be successful, and you will build a loyal partnership and accomplish more together.

If you are an alpha woman, how will you own your alpha and use more of your Value-Based Power to benefit others, your organization, society, and yourself?

If you are not an alpha woman, how will you advocate for alpha women taking on more positional power at home, at work, in your community organizations, and in society as a whole?

Master Subtle Strength

A downside of being an alpha can be the tendency to drive so fast you aren't paying attention to others. Mastering Subtle Strength can help you leverage your drive while bringing others along. As we learned in chapter 1, Subtle Strength is intentional influence that demonstrates calm confidence, backbone, and respect. Think of Subtle Strength as being strategically assertive rather than emotionally aggressive.

Use Value-Based Power in a Balanced Way

One challenge many alpha women have is a tendency to over-focus their power to support others, sometimes at the cost of their organization, society, and themselves. Using the Value-Based Power framework to make decisions can help make sure your power and influence are balanced.

Self. In *How Women Rise: Break the 12 Habits Holding You Back from Your Next Raise, Promotion, or Job*, authors and executive advisors Sally Helgesen and Marshall Goldsmith identify the self-sabotaging habits that tend to hold women back in the workplace and how to address them.[61] Two of these habits are a reluctance to claim your achievements and expecting others to spontaneously notice and reward your contributions, which indicate a lack of focus on self. On the other hand, several other habits—overvaluing expertise, putting your job before your career, and perfectionism—relate to overfocusing on self, at the cost of not investing enough power in what might benefit others, your organization, or society.

Others. Although women's strengths are in interpersonal relationships and all the nonverbal signals that go along with that, this strength can turn into a weakness if you overfocus on what will benefit others and your interpersonal relationships at the cost of what's best for yourself, your organization, or society. Helgesen and Goldsmith point out at least five habits related to overfocusing on interpersonal relationships, including "the disease to please," minimizing, emotionally "overreacting," ruminating, or letting your radar distract you.

Organization and Society. Two common habits—building rather than leveraging relationships and failing to build allies—relate to neglecting what would benefit the organization and society. Consider how strategic alliances can benefit your organization and society and how they can exponentially increase your influence for good in the areas that matter most to you.

If you find that you are out of balance related to Value-Based Power, return to the Value-Based Power worksheet (available for download at OnPointAdvising.com/BullyProof), where you can ask yourself valuable questions to shift in a positive direction.

Value-Based Power (VBP) Check-In

- Am I aware of the values, ambitions, and challenges in all four facets of VBP?
- Am I taking action across all four facets?

- If your answer to any part of these questions is no, then ask yourself the following two questions:
- How can I become more aware of the values, ambitions, and challenges in all four facets of VBP?
- What actions do I want to take to get closer to leveraging my VBP in a more balanced way?

Let's return to Trey, the executive who wanted to succeed as a leader but didn't want to get caught up in the dysfunctional power dynamics of her organization. We chose an approach that leveraged her Value-Based Power, where she was able to draw confidence in knowing that she was equally motivated to create success for herself, other people, the organization, and the greater good. She began to engage leveraging overt and Subtle Strength and even pointed out to the executive team when they were talking over her. It was a challenge, but over time more people on the executive team realized the unintentional negative impact of their usual ways of communicating.

BullyProof Strategy #9: Advocate for Alpha Women Leaders

1. Adapt to the culture without sacrificing your values.
2. Leverage Value-Based Power as your beacon for making decisions.
3. Integrate more overt and Subtle Strength.
4. Bring other women along with you.
5. Alpha women: Own your alpha.
6. Men: Commit to being an active partner rather than just aware of the challenge.
7. Men and women: Encourage all women to embrace their alpha and advocate for one another.

Given that women are naturally more collaborative and participative, it can catch some people off guard when women drive toward their ambitions. When it comes to success in work and life, my advice is the same for men and women. Who you are is who you are. What's just as important is being aware, adaptive, and intentionally influential. While there are differences between men and women, the best approach is integrating the natural strengths of *both* men and women. The more emerging leaders see women who are comfortable taking charge and who are aware adaptive alphas, the better chance we have of closing those gender gaps and achieving more business and social good together.

Awareness, Application, and Alliances

What insights did I have in this chapter?

What will I apply and when?

With whom will I share what I learned?

CHAPTER 10

Put People over Politics and Strengthen Society

*"Apologize for What?: Biden Doubles Down as
Segregation Scandal Escalates"*
Vanity Fair, June 20, 2019

"Trump Responds to Biden Remarks: I Don't Think I'm a Bully"
The Hill, July 5, 2019

"Ready to Rumble. U.S.-China Fight Puts World Economy on the Brink"
New York Times, August 6, 2019

The party doesn't matter. The source doesn't matter. The headline doesn't matter. What does matter? The underlying issue. In America, we let people in power have all the power.

Our society has never been more divided. We try to make ourselves feel better by allowing employees to have flex time or telling people diversity, inclusion, and equity is important. The truth is that weakness gets preyed on. Dominant people know what they want and get it. Weak people watch others get what they want.

Does this seem harsh? Maybe. But unless we can equip people with Subtle Strength and teach dominant people that they are losing more than they're gaining, nothing will change. Businesses can no longer hide. Executives must not only pay attention to how they treat their people; they must *take action* to help their teams, organization, and society become BullyProof.

Whether or not you're a leader, how can we all work toward creating more BullyProof organizations and strengthen society? In this chapter, we'll apply what we've learned about training our brain, Subtle Strength, and Value-Based Power to stop the bullying effects of partisan bias at home and at work, create alliances with the powerful and powerless, advocate for the underrepresented, create BullyProof brands and communities, and commit to causes that matter to us.

Stop Bullying Yourself

The first step toward creating a more BullyProof society is to stop bullying ourselves. What do I mean by that? In chapter 3, we discussed the power of cognitive biases. Nowhere are our biases more obvious than when we start talking about politics or social issues. An unaware brain can bully us into a reactive state, where our minds reject new information, lose access to empathy and strategic thinking, and view every disagreement as a threat. And we won't even realize it's happening.

Why are political and social topics so triggering? According to the research of Jay Van Bavel and his colleague Andrea Pereira at New York University, it has to do with the well-researched phenomenon of *social identity theory*, which states that people define who they are based at least partially on the groups they psychologically identify with.[62] From an evolutionary perspective, humans and other primates organized in groups for survival. Knowing who was in our group and who was outside our group helped us make quick decisions about when and who to sacrifice for (based on who we believed would sacrifice for us) to protect not just power and resources but a sense of belonging.[63]

For these reasons, our brains evolved to identify and quickly align with an *in-group* (a group we psychologically identify with) versus an *out-group* (a group we don't identify with).[64] Research has shown that we very quickly pattern our behavior and preferences based on the in-group norms, usually without realizing it. Our social identities also affect the way we interpret information, which affects the conclusions we draw and the beliefs we have.[65]

Our environment may look very different than that of our ancestors, but our brains haven't changed much. We're still scanning for who's in our group and who's out and behaving accordingly.

The problem, say Van Bavel and Pereira, is when this in-group/out-group behavior distorts our view of reality. Today's political parties are a prime example. If we have aligned with a political party as an in-group and that group is challenged (such as when watching a "biased" news source or talking with extended family), it can trigger a reactive state—which, as we learned in chapter 3, significantly affects our ability to process information and even objectively assess facts. According to Van Bavel's research, members of a political party are more likely to believe negative things about members of the other party, while they're more likely to give members of their own party the benefit of the doubt.[66]

Political parties can fulfill similar needs, such as belonging, power, material resources, and morality, as any tribal group. "To the extent that partisan identities fulfill these goals," say Van Bavel and Pereira, "they can generate a powerful incentive to distort beliefs in a manner that defies truth—especially when the net value of these goals outweighs accuracy goals."[67]

That point is worth repeating: if we deeply identify with a political group, we are likely to distort our beliefs in a manner that defies truth.

As just one example, in a TED-Ed talk Van Bavel shares a study where researchers gave a math test to 1,100 adults. As part of this math test, participants were asked two questions, each based on a data set that showed clear, objective answers to the questions.

Question 1: What is the correlation between rashes and a new skin cream?

Question 2: What is the correlation between crime rates and gun control legislation?

Participants with strong math skills were much more likely get the first question correct, but for the second question, participants' political identity significantly affected their likelihood of getting the question right. If their political beliefs happened to agree with what the data showed, they were much more likely to choose the correct answer. In fact, if the correct answer did not align with their political beliefs, even participants with the strongest math skills were 45 percent more likely to get the question incorrect![68]

How can this be? The reason, says Van Bavel, is *cognitive dissonance*, or the tension between two incompatible thoughts.[69] In this case, it's the data we see in the data set and our belief that our group is right. Our brain is driven to resolve cognitive dissonance no matter what, and if our commitment to our group is strong enough, that can mean closing our eyes to reality.

The overidentification with a group, or *partisan bias*, affects our memory: "Democrats were more likely than Republicans to incorrectly remember G.W. Bush on vacation during the Katrina hurricane, and Republicans were more likely than Democrats to falsely remember seeing Barack Obama shaking hands with the President of Iran."[70] It can even affect our values. People tend to prefer the policies of their political party even when those policies don't match their beliefs.[71]

This kind of partisan bias doesn't just happen with politics: it can apply to national identity, gender, race, ethnicity, food beliefs, sports teams—any type of group identity.

These studies tell us that no one is immune to the effects of partisanship. It doesn't matter how intellectually or emotionally intelligent you are: if you have strongly identified with a particular group, your brain will not *let* you see facts that challenge your group's beliefs. You will misremember events. And if a group leader states something that goes against your values, you may even end up changing your values without realizing it.

> Can you remember a time when your political/group identity bullied you into a triggered stress response, where you couldn't think openly and strategically? Did you ignore facts or change your values?

Left to its own devices, our brain bullies us with its biases, hiding facts, getting reactive, and putting us at a significant disadvantage when we have the opportunity to learn something new and create productive solutions.

So how can we combat our partisan bias and keep our brain from bullying us?

First, we can acknowledge that we all have partisan biases and likely have more biases than we realize.

Second, we can acknowledge that we can train our brain to go in the direction we want it to go rather than letting it run on autopilot.

Keep Your Partisan Bias from Bullying Yourself and Others

- **Be proactive.** When you feel passionate about a position, find facts, do your own research, and have conversations with people who see the world a different way.
- **Pause.** Don't debate or disagree until you truly hear what the other side is saying. Try not to let your emotions control you. When you hit pause, you are able to be more strategic.
- **Lead with Subtle Strength**. Once you have done your research and want to persuade someone else (especially another dominant person), take the following actions:
  - » Communicate with calm confidence, respect, and backbone.
  - » Pay attention to Motivational Currency and speak the other person's language.
  - » When stakes are high, leverage what you have learned from BRACE (bridging, respecting, aligning, challenging, and evidence) and DEALS (depersonalize, empathize, align, look for the hook, and show Subtle Strength).
- **Prioritize relationships**. Always do what you can to maintain the relationship and respect for one another.

Standing Up to Partisan Bullies at Home and at Work

Although the average citizen is likely unaware of the effects of their partisan biases, politicians are *very* aware of them. They *intentionally* use our partisan biases and in-group/out-group behavior to manipulate and bully us to achieve their own ends.

Politicians have trained us that integrity matters for everyone else except them. They lie, cheat, steal, and set people up for failure by intentionally tapping into our biases and triggers for their own gain. We not only expect it of them, we allow it to happen over and over.

In an environment like this, how can we influence partisan bullies, whether they're politicians or simply dominant people with strong opinions?

In the past, the general rule was not to talk about politics or social issues at work. The problem with this approach is that dominant people *are* talking about these issues, and avoiding or ignoring them simply causes the dominant person to assume you agree with them.

Gone are the days when we could hide from these conversations. Even if you choose not to engage, the conversation is coming to you.

If you want to use your power for good, the key is to neither avoid nor attack but to influence with overt and Subtle Strength. Remember that political issues have become so divisive because most people are on autopilot, controlled by their partisan biases. When our brain bullies us, we tend to bully others.

BullyProof Strategies for Positively Influencing Dominant People in Hot-Button Conversations

1. **Be clear.** In conversations with dominant people, you have to be clear or you lose power and agency.

2. **Set boundaries.** If there are topics that are off-limits with you, say so. Set up parameters and boundaries ahead of time. Or if the topic comes up, simply say you don't want to talk about that. You don't have to explain why; simply set the boundary.

3. **Use Value-Based Power.** When you align and leverage your value system, you have more courage to take action. For example, if someone is bullying you and you don't like conflict but you value empowering others, you will be more likely to do something about it. To help yourself connect to your values, consider all four areas of Value-Based Power: How does the situation impact self, others, organization, and society? And take action accordingly.

Advocate for the Underrepresented

The more we strengthen ourselves, the more we can strengthen others, particularly those underrepresented in leadership positions. For example, in the United States

- Black individuals are 13.4 percent of the population but 8 percent of managers and 3.8 percent of CEOs;[72]
- Hispanic individuals are 17 percent of the population but 4 percent of corporate executive positions in Fortune 500 companies;[73] and
- women are 50.8 percent of the population but 5 percent of CEO positions in Fortune 500 companies and 7.8 percent of CEO positions in S&P 500 companies.[74]

With 80 percent of Americans believing diversity in the workplace is important,[75] many companies are investing in Diversity, Equity, and Inclusion (DEI) initiatives, an important step toward empowering all people, including those who have been underrepresented. But you don't want the *way* you advocate to become a bigger story than *what* you're advocating for. Using a dominant approach, even when advocating for the underrepresented, typically backfires. For example, my primary experience of the Occupy Wall Street movement was walking down Wall Street with clients and getting yelled at. I wasn't sure what their intentions were because I kept hearing inconsistent messages. As far as I could see, they were only effective at making my walk to work five minutes longer.

The BullyProof strategies you've been learning not only help support DEI initiatives but allow them to be more powerful and sustainable. For example, using Subtle Strength and overt strength to influence others are more effective methods than dominance or submission. Balancing your influence with Value-Based Power and the high-stakes strategies of BRACE and DEALS helps teach people to appreciate differences. And leveraging Motivational Currency moves people toward understanding before commanding.

When I knew I wanted to take on some of the tougher aspects of biases in the workplace and the home, I reached out to Carmen Blanco, senior director of Equity, Inclusion, and Diversity at Tapestry, whose brands include Coach and Kate Spade. Carmen is a Latina woman who is and was a successful and seasoned leader in several corporations including MTV, Nickelodeon, Univision, and Harman. I have learned a lot from partnering with her over the years. What I appreciate most is her willingness to have conversations with me and others where we can ask a question without judgment and learn from her experiences. I could fill a whole chapter based on our conversations, but for now we will go with some of the most critical highlights.

Carmen's path is unique and has played a role in her ability to be an influential leader and help organizations take action on diversity and inclusion initiatives. She said early on she faced bias as she progressed in her career but didn't realize it. Carmen came up through the City University of New York (as the first college graduate in her family) and was in a business where many people came from Ivy League institutions and had the benefit of unpaid internships through their legacy networks. Consequently, she experienced in-group/out-group bias, but she didn't realize its impact at the time. She was just grateful to be there.

Carmen shared that Latino families place a high premium on nurturing and being there for their children, and, culturally, it is completely acceptable (and almost expected) that some sort of sacrifice was required, at least back then. As a result, her maternal instinct kicked in and she wanted to be there for her children. In the corporate world, that created a great deal of emotional labor because, at that time, maternal bias was prevalent in the industry. She did what many women did, which was work harder and longer to perform at a high level. The advice she got from executives was, "If my wife can do it, you can do it. Just get a nanny." You can imagine how that might impact someone. She overspent on education, volunteered for everything, and overworked herself. She also decided to subdue her identity as a mother at work: there were no family pictures, no leaving early to take kids to the doctor, no sharing about weekends with family, nothing that would risk others' perception of her as anything other than a professional.

It's so critical for us to be aware of our impact on others, especially if we are in positions of power. I couldn't help thinking about what happens to people who are not as insightful, intelligent, strong, caring, and gifted as Carmen.

I asked Carmen what she was working on at Tapestry. I could sense the excitement and hope in her voice. She has a lot going on and is making an impact. One very positive initiative is the creation of a Faith-Based Fact Sheet, which helps people in the organization be more aware of what different faiths believe and what is important to them. She also shared that businesses are not able to take on everything and need to be smart and selective about what initiatives they advocate for or support. The most important thing a company can do is level the playing field by addressing the systems, policies, and lack of transparency that have inadvertently kept opportunity out of reach for historically marginalized communities. Leveling the playing field will actually benefit everyone. It's not DEI work; it's the right thing to do for the modern workforce. Plus the modern workforce demands it! Carmen has also contributed to an assessment measure for an inclusion index that has four primary factors:

1. Feeling like you belong
2. Feeling safe to speak up without fear of negative consequence
3. How you perceive visible commitment from leadership
4. How frequently leaders empower you

Given Carmen's path and insights, I asked her what we can do to decrease bias and bullying, and create alliances.

Here is what she shared:

Allies will be more impactful if they fully ground themselves, have genuine curiosity, and want to lift others. We need people in executive positions to use their privilege and proximity to power to be active advocates for those who would not otherwise have a voice. Being inactive and an ally doesn't work; you're simply a bystander, or worse, a performative ally. I want advocates to center the people they are trying to help in their day-to-day lives and try to clear the barriers and influence the system. We need it to be less risky for people to advocate and be active. Lived experience is very different than learned experience. A White or male ally may only have learned experience, and that's okay. People who learn about bias rather than experience it can benefit by learning how to use their privilege to center others rather than themselves. People with lived experience are often times the best allies/confidants/ sounding boards to others who have had similar experiences. There is a built-in safe space that is low risk because you share a lived experience, and that is empowering to both parties.

For people who are navigating bias, find allies to partner with and escalate when needed. Find people in your network who can help you absorb the emotional labor.

Carmen clearly gets it and is helping people like me and others get it. As she told me, "It's not a shortage of talent; it's a shortage of opportunity." My conversation with Carmen made me even more motivated to learn about and take action on being an advocate.

Create an Alliance Mindset and Skill Set

One of the most common things I hear when talking with businesses about advocating for others is, "I'm not sure what I can do." There is a lot we can do. As we extend our influence, we will want to create alliances with not just the powerful but the powerless. That's how we strengthen society: we bring people up with us. One way to begin is to shift from a traditional mindset to an alliance mindset.

The graphic below illustrates the shift from a traditional mindset to an alliance mindset in more detail.

Figure 10.1. Traditional versus Alliance Mindset

As an example, let's say we want to help close the gender gap at our workplace. In the traditional mindset, the focus is on the past and the self and is set. The primary desire is to be comfortable and correct. As a result, we might make the following mistakes:

- People introduce women based on their characteristics, such as how many kids they have, rather than their contributions.
- Leaders give less feedback to women, and when they do it's full of clichés.
- Executives expect women to take on gender initiatives.

In an alliance mindset, the focus is on the future and the collective and is adaptive. The desire is to challenge self and others and to partner together. These results then follow:

- Women are viewed based on contributions.
- Feedback is individualized and based on performance and growth.
- Both men and women take on gender initiatives.

Khadijah Sharif-Drinkard, senior vice president of Business Affairs at ABC News, is a great example of what it means to have balanced VBP, Subtle Strength, and an alliance mindset. A lawyer by training, she has served brands such as Nickelodeon, BET, and Viacom. She continues to be a positive force in the media and entertainment world.

Over the years I have been fortunate to see Khadijah lead, influence, and be an advocate and mentor to many. Her drive for excellence is balanced with her drive for purpose and elevating others.

As a Black Muslim woman in the media industry, Khadijah acknowledges that she has experienced bias in a number of ways.

She also came to the business differently, in that she came into the industry straight out of law school.

"If you get trained outside the normal way of the business, people view you differently and you need to prove yourself," she said. "The people who weren't sure about me weren't against me, but they were biased."

When I asked her how she overcame that bias, she shared that her upbringing was key to overcoming obstacles, not just at work but in all of life.

"I was born into a situation where I had to work harder. When I hear the nos and experience bias, it motivates me to overcome and push through. When I was born, God didn't create me because I was deserving, but because I was deserving of more. Even though I had many challenges, I somehow knew I would belong and achieve excellence.

"So when I entered the media industry, I overperformed. I built credibility by taking on the most difficult assignments and the things people didn't want to do. I became the go-to person. I learned the rules of the union guilds and became a sought-after resource. I also became close with the people who didn't believe in me."

She influences alphas and strong personalities by being strong herself.

"I win them over. I'm very intentional," she said. "I come in with a sense of strength and the intention of being clear and direct. I don't get dominated, and I don't dominate. Although I have seen alphas be dominant in a way that doesn't suck the life out of the room.

"If I'm talking to someone who already has their mind made up, I set up preconversations to find out what they value. All alphas are not the same; they're motivated by different things. Some people just want it straight."

For those experiencing bias, here is Khadijah's advice:

"First, separate yourself from the value other people are placing on you. Too often we take on things people say as if they are true. If we internalize other people's feelings of us, we may become that very thing. Then, identify the bias and understand why it exists. For example, some people fear losing power. Understand the politics of it. Then ask, What can I do to create a situation where this bias can be eradicated?"

Khadijah points out that the ones experiencing the bias don't always have to be the ones teaching people not to be biased. "Decide if you need to take it on, or not. That decision takes some work and reflection. Ask yourself, What do you want to achieve?"

For people who want to eradicate their own biases, Khadijah recommends spending time walking in the shoes of people who aren't like them. "People in power need to invite others in more," she said. "Give people space to learn. Also, don't invite me to the party and let me sit on the floor. Dance with me."

When I asked her how we can build an alliance mindset and strengthen society, she said, "People help me, so I want to help others. I am a gap filler: I look for a need that is not being met, and I meet it. I ask, 'What do people need?' Even people with bias need something. COVID-19 taught us that people need people. We all need human connection.

"I believe our rent to pay on this earth is to help people see their potential. It may just be a kind word to someone. I watched my mother get a nursing degree while raising me and my three siblings. She had three bouts of cancer and still got her master's. There is potential for anything, even if you have to take one class at a time."

Her additional points about strengthening society can benefit us all:

- Have a cause or purpose outside of your job.
- See yourself as a server of people.
- Be an advocate for people who don't have a voice.
- See the underdog as a winner: David can win over Goliath.
- See power and potential in all people.
- Don't write anyone off—we are all winners.

Find a Cause

We all have our default focus, whether it's self-improvement, meeting others' needs, maximizing productivity and profit, or another priority. Yet overfocusing on one area, no matter how positive that area is, can result in wrong decisions or being out of balance. The more balanced our focus across all four areas of Value-Based Power, the less negative things impact us.

For example, during the peak of COVID-19, my business went down 61 percent. But because I had a nonprofit, a family, friends who needed assistance in other areas, and a book project to work on, I felt good about what I was focused on and had a purpose outside of profit alone.

This is one great reason to find a cause to support. Not only does it help draw your focus toward others, organization, and society, it adds positive purpose to your life. Even better, if you are a leader of a group, committing to a cause as an organization can be very motivating and inspirational for your entire team. Many companies have chosen to give a percentage of their time, money, and energy to a cause that is meaningful for them—including Morgan James Publishing, the publisher of this book. One of the reasons I'm proud to publish with Morgan James is that they give a percentage of their profits to Habitat for Humanity.

> What cause are you drawn to support? What action will you take to move in that direction?

Build a BullyProof Brand

When we hear the word "brand," we often think of large companies that spend millions of dollars on creating a connection to their customers and communities. The reason it's worth the investment is a brand creates loyalty and gives people a sense of confidence that they know what they are getting. The same is true for you as an individual. Whether you know it or not, you have a brand, so you might as well be intentional about what message your brand is sending.

I have found that bullies are less likely to bully people who have a personal brand that includes being willing to influence others and not being willing to be submissive or dominant. Also, people who have alliances with people who have BullyProof brands are less likely to get pushed around. Building a brand is just like any other worthwhile endeavor; it takes time, energy, focus, and intention.

I wanted to learn more about branding and increasing my visibility on LinkedIn, so I applied to work with Dr. Natalia Wiechowski, who is a branding consultant, keynote speaker, and LinkedIn expert. She has over 110,000 followers on LinkedIn. Her advice and coaching has paid dividends and led me to create partnerships with other like-minded professionals. Dr. Nat has many gifts, one of them being able to connect with a diverse range of people and gently nudging them to take on their challenges and grow.

I wanted to get her perspective on building a brand and how a BullyProof brand can be a valuable tool. Here are my questions (in italics), and her answers.

What are the first steps for creating a brand?

The first step is getting clarity. Design the space and time to deeply ponder who you truly are, what you have to offer, and how you want to live and work.

If you don't understand yourself, chances are high that your fellow coworkers, suppliers, clients, friends, and family don't understand you either. Here are a few guiding questions to begin with:

- What kind of issue do I solve? (Every job solves a problem.)
- For whom do I solve that problem? (This is your customer/employer avatar.)
- What does my customer get as a result?
- When do they get the result?
- Why should people choose me and not my competition?
- How would I like to be perceived? (e.g., as powerful, funny, smart, kind)
- What are my three core values? (e.g., freedom, family, time)
- How do I want people to feel when they are around me? (e.g., safe, seen, inspired, heard, empowered)

By the way, in branding lingo, what we've just done is called positioning. And yes, getting clearer on these questions is a journey, so be compassionate towards yourself but also have the courage to reflect on these aspects.

How does having a brand help you when interacting with challenging people or bullies?

First of all, you have a brand whether you like it or not. Because, as Jeff Bezos has said, "Your brand is what people say about you when you are not in the room." For me, a brand is career insurance, and a self-leadership and communications tool. So, the big question here is, do you

1. have a clear brand, one that helps you reach your targets, or

2. is your communication messy or all over the place?

Let's assume you have done the (inner) work and clearly positioned yourself. In this process, you will have learned a lot about yourself. Maybe you will also have discovered thought patterns or a specific behavior that doesn't serve you anymore.

The just mentioned new insights have the potential to empower you to set healthy personal boundaries and say "no, thank you" in a respectful and graceful way. Because now you are finally aware of the value you bring to the table. In other words, with this newly gained self-confidence, you might tolerate less nonsense.

You could even conclude that the behavior of challenging people is not happening to you but for you. It isn't there to hurt you, but to show you an area of needed personal change that could result in immense growth.

I, for example, used to attract many "terrible" bosses and clients into my life who made me feel unworthy and incompetent, until I finally understood—not on an intellectual level, but in every cell of my body—that I am enough. I don't attract such situations into my life anymore. And in the rare cases that such individuals cross my path, their behavior does not trigger me anymore.

When you can smile about the bully's behavior and feel compassion for the unnecessary, childlike drama they create, you know you've evolved to the next level of self-awareness and inner peace. Kudos!

What advice or suggestions do you have for people looking to create a brand that deters people from trying to push them around?

Decide to make your physical, emotional, mental, and spiritual health a priority. Now, I am not telling you to turn into a selfish, arrogant, cold dork here. I'm inviting you to commit to, look after, and care for yourself. To sort of marry yourself first. Because you cannot pour tea to serve others from an empty teapot. The way you treat yourself sets the path for how others treat you.

If you find that difficult, that's okay; gift yourself with an accountability partner who will support you on that journey. An expert who has been in your situation before and who now lives and works in a way that is aligned with your vision of your best self. Remember: Never take advice from someone who isn't where or how you'd like to be! Would you accept parenting advice from someone who isn't a parent? You wouldn't. The same is true for other aspects for your life and career.

Some mental patterns, routines, or concepts we have about ourselves and the world are deeply wired into us, so deeply that we are not aware of them. And if we are, it might be difficult to get rid of them on our own. In Germany, where I am originally from, we have the saying, "A trouble shared is a trouble halved." So, allow yourself to have a gentler inner transformation. Change can be tough enough. Why do it on your own if you can have a "partner in crime" who cheers for you and wants you to succeed?

I can tell you firsthand I have seen Dr. Nat help the most resistant people push through their discomfort and build brands that send off the message they are BullyProof. I continue to follow her work and learn.

Build BullyProof Communities

As we use these BullyProof strategies at home, at work, and with our other organizations, we create BullyProof communities.

For example, maybe you believe there should be more mentoring in your organization. You begin sharing your ideas with others, and you realize you're not alone. You begin meeting together as a group and create coalitions with other aligned groups in your community. You have now built a BullyProof community focused on a common goal.

The Power of Mentors

According to our research, one of the easiest and most impactful things you can do is help a person set up a professional relationship with someone they admire.

- People with mentors are more confident, think they're more influential, are more willing to do hard things like have difficult conversations when needed, are more satisfied with life, are more engaged at work, and associate with success.
- People who reported having a mentor or leader whom they admired were more likely to experience the following:
  » Communication confidence
  » Overall confidence
  » The perception they can influence others
  » Willingness to engage in hard conversations
  » Life satisfaction
  » Employee engagement
  » The perception they were currently successful

One challenge new groups often face is what to do when people disagree and there are no standard practices yet. A good strategy is to create principles and guidelines to follow for standard procedures, such as running a meeting, to help defuse the emotion in a situation. When you can return to the guidelines you decided on as a group, conflicts can often be solved before they start.

You can also create BullyProof communities within groups you're already part of. Let's say we're in the midst of the COVID-19 pandemic and you have a family member at home who is immunocompromised. You're very conservative about social distancing and wearing masks for the sake of your family member, although you consider yourself to be reasonable when it comes to assessing risk.

Let's say you're also a member of the PTA at a school with a strict mask-wearing policy indoors. When you arrive at tonight's meeting, you notice that none of the parents are wearing masks.

What would you do? Would you leave? Bring it to someone's attention? Announce that everyone should follow school protocol and put on masks? Stay in the room and say nothing?

If you wanted to take a BullyProof approach, you might do the following.

First, you could assess the situation from the perspective of Value-Based Power. How does this situation of no mask-wearing impact you, others in the room, your other family members, your organization, and/or society?

Based on that assessment, you could mentally use the DEALS process to defuse any potential bombs.

Depersonalize: Realize the fact that they're not wearing masks is not personal to you.

Empathize: Consider what situations might lead someone to choose not to wear masks in this instance and consider their goals for this meeting.

Align: Find something you can all agree on as a place to begin.

Look for the hook: Wait for an opportunity to bring the issue up with minimal disruption.

Show Subtle Strength: The president asks if anyone has anything relevant they'd like to share, and with Subtle Strength, you calmly and clearly say the following:

"I have a question about wearing masks during our meetings. I know we're all here to support our children and we don't want to be overly fearful. But I'm in a situation where I need to wear a mask, and I'd like to know what the parameters are just so we can all know what to expect. Could we decide together on what our practice will be?"

Showing up this way strengthens your shared mission, helps defuse conflict before it starts, and models BullyProof behavior in your community, allowing it to ripple out and strengthen society.

BullyProof Strategy #10: Put People over Politics and Strengthen Society

1. Recognize your potential partisan biases and train your brain to keep them from bullying you.
2. Stand up to partisan bullies with Subtle Strength.
3. Advocate for the underrepresented and create opportunities for them.
4. Create alliances with the powerful and the powerless.
5. Find a cause.
6. Build a BullyProof personal brand.
7. Build BullyProof communities, one conversation at a time.

We can model BullyProof behavior in any group, whether it's at work, at home, in our sports teams, or any other community organization. As we strengthen ourselves, others, our organizations, and our communities, we strengthen society, one conversation at a time.

Awareness, Application, and Alliances

What insights did I have in this chapter?

What will I apply and when?

With whom will I share what I learned?

CHAPTER 11

Finish with HOW

once worked with a professional athlete who believed he was on the same level as Michael Jordan and Kobe Bryant. He could clearly articulate why he was going to play at an elite level and was obsessed with visualizing himself playing against elite players. Unfortunately, it wasn't enough: he was never able to reach the level he believed he was capable of. He got too focused on what it would feel like to be elite and why he would become elite, and he didn't pay attention to *how* he would become elite.

We fail to plan for what makes us fail. Individuals and organizations are obsessed with being positive, uncovering their why, and writing vision statements. While these serve a purpose and are all enjoyable to experience, talk about, and even write down, they are first steps, not final steps. Often, they set us up for failure because a plan that does not specifically include how we are going to get where we want to go and what may get in the way gives us a false sense of confidence in achieving our goals. An overemphasis on *why* without *how* can actually decrease our performance.

And while imagery can be powerful, visualizing a successful performance without planning how you are going to get to that level of performance is sure to have you come up short.

On this journey, you've received many tools and strategies to become BullyProof for yourself, for others, for your organization, and for society at large. I invited you to see how the most effective way to influence is through Subtle Strength and Value-Based Power. You've also been offered strategies on how to keep your brain from bullying you, to appreciate the strengths and limitations of alphas, to use Motivational Currency at work and home, to BRACE for impact, to make DEALS with alphas when stakes are high, and to become a more effective ally and advocate for the underrepresented in your organization and your community.

Now the question is, What's next for you?

Whatever strategy you want to implement, taking a stand for Value-Based Power for all people—including ourselves—is powerful and inspiring work. Whether we are in positions of power or not, we all have the ability to create positive experiences that are contagious. At the same time, negativity is also contagious, and as we've discovered, it can lead to many dysfunctional outcomes and challenges. The more we take intentional action toward becoming BullyProof and staying aligned with VBP, the greater our chances of elevating ourselves and others. I believe that too often we sit back and let things happen and that often puts us into the victim mentality. The journey of becoming BullyProof has massive physical, financial, and psychological rewards.

But no matter how powerful your vision is, it means very little if you never take action.

No matter how powerful your why is, *why* without *how* falls short.

I would never say writing this book was easy. But I will say that it is far easier to offer a new point of view or teach a new framework than it is to get people to change their behavior and create new habits.

What we know from data on presentations and training is that we forget within days the large majority of what is presented. Theories based on the Ebbinghaus Forgetting Curve, which date back to 1885, suggest that when we learn something new, we only retain approximately 40 percent of the information after just a few days.[76] I have seen a large percentage of people who set goals fail and often times stop setting goals because they don't see progress and lose focus.

Based on my experience, here are common mistakes I've seen related to professional development:

- We focus on too many areas at one time.
- We're overconfident about our ability to remember what we have learned.
- We do not plan for obstacles.
- We believe in myths, such as if you simply state your vision often enough, it will come true.
- We fail to engage others in our process.

Becoming BullyProof is an elite goal, and it will require elite training. You need a plan for what's next.

Success is not based on wishful thinking but on strength.

In this chapter, you will learn why *how* is important, plan for obstacles, and create a personal strategy to become BullyProof with a bias toward action so you can make your BullyProof vision a reality.

Why How Matters

The critical predictor of your success is what you choose to believe. Beliefs are extremely powerful, and we need to be aware of how they drive our behaviors. We hear a lot about how our limiting beliefs, such as believing we can't do something, can cause us to fail. Yet our beliefs that are not based in reality can also cause us to fail. For example, believing that my vision will happen simply because I want it to happen drives complacency rather than taking the actions that will actually allow me to achieve my vision.

On the other hand, when we plan for the how and have an accurate picture of what needs to happen to achieve our vision, our beliefs become even more powerful. According to the research of Albert Bandura, focusing on how to accomplish a task increases a person's self-efficacy, or the belief in their ability to accomplish a task.

Also, in a study by psychologists Lien Pham and Shelley Taylor at the University of California, one group of students was asked to visualize the positive end result of receiving a good grade for a few minutes each day as they prepared for a midterm exam, while another group had the same midterm exam but was not asked to visualize anything. Both groups tracked the hours they spent studying. This visualization had a significant effect on both the hours these students spent studying as well as their score but not in the way you may expect. The first group *studied less* and had *lower grades* than the second group. The visualizing may have made them feel good, but it had negative effects on their actual results.

Interestingly, there was also a third group in this study, and those participants were asked to visualize *how* they were going to get a high grade on the midterm for a few minutes each day. In comparison to the first and second groups, this group studied more hours and earned higher grades than both groups. Pham and

Taylor concluded that visualizing the detailed steps of how they would achieve their vision prepared them better for success.[77]

According to neuroscientist Tali Sharot's research, it has to do with how our brain is wired. In her TED Talk on the optimism bias, Sharot shares that we tend to believe negative situations are less likely to happen to us and positive situations are more likely to happen to us regardless of the actual likelihood of that event. To illustrate, she used a cartoon where penguins are poised at the edge of a cliff. The optimistic penguins believe they can fly, while the pessimistic penguins do not. However, optimism isn't enough, as shown by the penguins jumping off the cliff to their demise. There is one penguin wearing a parachute, however, who safely made it to the ground. This optimistic penguin thought about the *how*, and he had far more success than both the optimistic penguins who didn't prepare and the pessimistic penguins who never even tried.[78]

Similarly, in her book *Rethinking Positive Thinking*, Gabriele Oettingen makes the case that we have been setting goals incorrectly: according to the past twenty years of research in the area of human motivation, people tend to fail because they fail to plan for obstacles.

To account for the science of goal setting, Oettingen created a process called WOOP: Wish, Outcome, Obstacle, Plan. The wish is what you want, the outcome is the positive result of fulfilling your wish, the obstacle is what will likely get in the way of achieving your wish, and your plan is how you will overcome your obstacle. According to Oettingen's research, planning for obstacles with a process like WOOP resulted in reduced stress, increased engagement at work, improved problem-solving, increased weight loss, healthier relationships, and improved school performance.[79]

Addressing the how is the difference between failure and peak performance. I had the privilege of speaking at a large company in San Francisco about mental toughness. At the end of my talk, I introduced San Francisco 49ers Hall of Famer Ronnie Lott. He was known for his toughness. He shared a story of meeting Navy SEALs and talking with them about their preparation prior to battle. Lott thought it would be something similar to being in the locker room with the team and getting amped up for a football game. What he learned was that many Navy SEALs sleep in the helicopters on the way to their missions. The reason being, he shared, was that they were so focused and well prepared with planning for obstacles and how they would carry out the mission that the best strategy was to be calm and confident.

When Michael Phelps's goggles broke and filled with water during the Beijing Olympics in 2008, he was able to not only finish but earn a gold medal because he knew exactly how many strokes he needed to complete each lap. In fact, he won eight gold medals in Beijing that year—not just because he had immense talent and believed he could do it but also because he practiced the how and planned day after day for potential obstacles.[80]

What you want is important. Why you want it is also important, but it doesn't give you a strategy for getting what you want. What you believe is important, but it's not enough on its own. If results matter to you, *how* is the most important.

Finish with HOW

If you're serious about becoming BullyProof, it's time to focus on how. Here is a simple approach to focus on HOW to become BullyProof, where HOW stands for *habits, obstacles,* and *way forward.*

Habits

Habits are what happen when we're not thinking. There are two kinds of habits: the behaviors that move us away from what we want and the behaviors that move us closer to what we want. Our habits create our experience, so if we're not having the experience we want, becoming aware of what moves us further from or propels us closer toward what we want allows us to take intentional action.

For example, let's say a CEO had a direct report who was an alpha and a bully. The CEO came prepared to meetings with a clear vision and desired outcome, but his report consistently took over the meetings and all decisions went her way. The CEO wanted to become more BullyProof, increase his influence in his interactions with this person, and lead meetings more effectively.

His first step was to consider what habits were moving him away from the outcomes he wanted. One of those habits was to be agreeable and maintain harmony when anyone disagreed with him. In his mind, he wanted to welcome all voices and be collaborative, but it was causing him to lose credibility with the team.

Now he considered which new habits might bring him closer to his outcome. He thought about the Value-Based Power model, and he recognized that simply allowing his report to redirect the meeting might be serving him, but it wasn't serving the other team members or the company. This realization strengthened his resolve to change his behavior and show up with Subtle Strength to benefit others and the organization.

Instead, his new habit would be to lean into the discomfort and use overt and Subtle Strength to redirect the team back to his original agenda. Whenever she engaged and attempted to redirect, he could still use his natural strength of agreeing first, but he could also build a new habit of influencing using Subtle Strength to better balance his Value-Based Power.

> What habits are moving you away from what you want?
>
> What habits are moving you toward what you want?

Obstacles

Changing our habits can be challenging, but it's not impossible—especially if we're aware of our obstacles.

Our obstacles are our thoughts, feelings, or behaviors that get in the way of what we want. When we focus on HOW, we focus on our *internal* obstacles (the things under our control) because our internal obstacles drive our habits. Focusing on what we can control also keeps us in the ownership cycle (see chapter 1).

The CEO thought about the internal obstacle driving his habit of allowing his report to redirect meetings, and he realized it was his discomfort with conflict, especially with an alpha personality who typically insisted on her own way, that influenced his response.

> What internal obstacles are likely to get in the way of doing what you need to do?
>
> What thoughts, feelings, or behaviors drive the habits that take you away from what you want?

Way Forward

The way forward means creating a strategy to set new habits that get you where you want to go while also planning for obstacles.

Remember what happens to our brain under stress: when we get thrown into fight or flight, we lose access to our higher brain and get more tactical than strategic. Also, according to the research of Tali Sharot and her colleagues, people who are experiencing threat need less evidence to decide they are in an undesirable situation, which creates a steady stream of inaccurate decisions.[81]

In other words, when we're experiencing threat, we think things are worse than they actually are. Remind yourself this is going to happen and be prepared.

Use the following methods to plan for obstacles in a stressful interaction:

- **Feelings forecast**. When you know the weather forecast, you can prepare. Getting caught in a rainstorm is much better when you have an umbrella and a raincoat. Same rain, different impact. Knowing what you know about the situation, how can you prepare for the "storm"?
- **If/then role-play**. Ask a trusted colleague or friend to practice role-playing specific situations and talk them through. Focus the conversation on, "If X happens, then I will do or say Y." Get feedback and advice and repeat until you are confident in your approach and have thought through at least three scenarios.
- **Reality check**. Ask yourself, "Who is this conversation about? Me, the other person, or both?"

By moving forward and setting new habits, we're training our brain to follow our lead—to do what's necessary rather than what's comfortable. The key is to focus internally on what you can control rather than on external situations you can't control.

To create your way forward, list three to five intentional actions that will address the obstacles you identified and will take you where you want to go.

For example, to address his internal obstacles and create a new habit that would move him closer to his desired outcome of more effectively leading meetings with his direct report in the room, the CEO chose the following intentional actions:

1. He would prepare some statements ahead of time to help him redirect a conversation, ensuring he was confident, prepared, and ready to go into the meeting.
2. He would practice redirecting using if/then role-plays with a trusted colleague.
3. He would have a direct conversation with his report about what he hoped to accomplish in future meetings.
4. He would continue to work on his own confidence and comfort level when disagreeing with others by practicing with friends and colleagues in small-stakes situations.

List three to five intentional actions that will address the obstacles you identified and will move you closer to where you want to go.

Now you can rearrange HOW into *who*: "Who is going to help me with my HOW?" We have all heard people say relationships are the most important part of life and work. It's true, and the more you put effort into building, repairing, and nurturing relationships, the more return on your effort you will get.

One key is to build relationships before you need them. A time-tested strategy in building relationships is asking people for advice and engaging them in your growth. People naturally want to help others succeed, and high performers love giving advice. Be mindful of how time intensive your asks are and diversify the types of people you invite to support your journey. One approach is to think of four people who are each motivated by one of the four core motivators of Motivational Currency: Performance, People, Power, and Purpose.

> Who will help you identify habits, recognize likely obstacles, and chart a way forward?

HOW to Become BullyProof

Now it's your turn to create your personal strategy for becoming BullyProof, to include the what, the why, the when, the HOW, and the who.

First, let's review all the strategies we've covered:

BullyProof Strategy #1: Own Your Power

1. If you find yourself caught in a victim mentality, choose to enter the ownership cycle by accepting the situation rather than rejecting or resisting it.
2. Use the Value-Based Power framework as a checklist for your next decision or to evaluate a recent interaction. How balanced is your influence?
3. Take the Strength Styles quiz and identify your default strength style.

BullyProof Strategy #2: Identify the Alpha

1. When you're having trouble influencing someone in a positive way, review the Alpha Quiz. Is this person an alpha?

2. If this person is an alpha, review the four types of alphas on the Alpha Matrix. What type are they?
3. The next time you interact with this person, use one of the recommended strength styles on the Alpha Matrix for that type.

BullyProof Strategy #3: Train Your Brain

1. Recognize how your brain can bully you through stress reactions, shortcuts, and biases.
2. Use deliberate practice to train your brain to shift from a reactive or biased state to a more intentional state.
3. To avoid triggering the bully in others, influence with empathy and hope rather than pressure or fear.

BullyProof Strategy #4: Recognize, Read, and Lead with Motivational Currency

Choose someone you want to influence or build a greater relationship with and follow these steps.

1. Recognize your Motivational Currency. To verify, take the Motivational Currency Calculator (MCC) at OnPointAdvising.com/MotivationalCurrency.
2. Read others' Motivational Currency with the Coins of Motivational Currency.
3. Lead by adapting to align with their Motivational Currency, using tools like the Motivation Map to support your learning and strategy.

BullyProof Strategy #5: BRACE for Impact

1. *Bridge* to connect with empathy and understanding.
2. *Respect* to allow space for the other person to talk through their perspective.

3. *Align* to find common ground among ambitions and priorities and cocreate collective insights.
4. *Challenge* to share your point of view with confidence and assertiveness.
5. Use *evidence* to back up your statements with data.

BullyProof Strategy #6: Defuse the Bomb

When an alpha has become a bully, make DEALS with them:
1. *Depersonalize* to shift from reactive to intentional.
2. *Empathize* to connect with the bully's situation and do something they might not expect.
3. *Align* to reflect understanding of their position to lower tension and increase comfort.
4. *Look for the hook* to find the opportunity to agree and move forward.
5. *Show Subtle Strength* to demonstrate respect and backbone.

BullyProof Strategy #7: Minimize Bullying Behaviors

1. Take the Bully Barometer.
2. Use the Emotional Intelligence in Action framework to decrease bullying behaviors.
3. Use the Value-Based Power framework to increase building behaviors.

BullyProof Strategy #8: Practice Growth Leadership in Times of Crisis

1. Commit to growing through crisis and helping your organization do the same.
2. Take the GTAS to learn about yourself and build your growth skills.
3. Use the Value-Based Power framework to set your focus.

4. Use the SPEAKERS framework to know what to do during a crisis.

5. Use the Five Keys for Growth Leadership to implement how to do it.

BullyProof Strategy #9: Advocate for Alpha Women Leaders

1. Adapt to the culture without sacrificing your values.
2. Leverage Value-Based Power as your beacon for making decisions.
3. Integrate more overt and Subtle Strength.
4. Bring other women along with you.
5. Alpha women: Own your alpha.
6. Men: Commit to being an active partner rather than just aware of the challenge.
7. Men and women: Encourage women to embrace their alpha and advocate for one another.

BullyProof Strategy #10: Put People over Politics and Strengthen Society

1. Recognize your potential partisan biases and train your brain to keep it from bullying you.
2. Stand up to partisan bullies with Subtle Strength.
3. Advocate for the underrepresented and create opportunities for them.
4. Create alliances with the powerful and the powerless.
5. Find a cause.
6. Build a BullyProof personal brand.
7. Build BullyProof communities, one conversation at a time.

Think back to the reason you first picked up this book.

Why did you want to become more BullyProof? What challenge were you facing or what did you want to achieve? What impact did you want to make?

Now that you've reached the end of this book, what do you want to accomplish most?

If you successfully accomplished this, what difference would it make for you, for the people you care about, for your organization, for society?

What I want to accomplish	
Why I want to accomplish it	
When I want to accomplish it	
Finish with *HOW*: Habits, Obstacles, Way Forward	
Habits that take me away from my objective	
Habits that take me closer to my objective	
Obstacles (Internal)	

Way Forward	
Who will help me with my HOW?	

Figure 11.1. HOW to Become BullyProof

Consider where you would like to start in becoming Bul-lyProof. Would you like to start with yourself, your team, your organization, or your community? What new behavior would you establish in that area? For best results, focus on just one BullyProof behavior at a time.

Then fill out the chart above. You can download an editable copy at https://onpointadvising.com/bullyproof/.

What, Why, and When

Write down what you want to accomplish, why you want to accomplish it, and by when you want to accomplish it.

HOW

Next, write down HOW you will accomplish it.

Habits. List the habits or behaviors that are moving you *away* from your objective and the habits or behaviors that are moving you *closer* to your objective.

Obstacles. Now consider your internal obstacles. What thoughts, feelings, or behaviors drive the habits taking you away from your objective? Why are you taking the actions you are taking? Focus on the internal obstacles under your control rather than obstacles in others or in your environment that are beyond your control.

Way forward. Now that you are aware of the habits you want to stop, the habits you want to increase, and the internal obstacles that will likely trip you up as you work on changing your habits, you can plan a way forward.

Write down three to five intentional actions that address your obstacles and will lead you toward your new BullyProof behavior.

Who

Write down who will help you with your HOW. If no one comes to mind, try the approach suggested earlier: think of four people each motivated by one of the four core motivators of Motivational Currency (Performance, People, Power, and Purpose).

Once you achieve this BullyProof objective, set a new one and repeat the process.

Tips for Changing Your Habits

Although changing our habits is challenging, it's not impossible. Here are some tips to increase your chances of success.

- Build one BullyProof behavior at a time.

- Rather than adding more to your plate, integrate your new habit into what you're already doing, such as leading a meeting or creating a new presentation.
- Create an image or metaphor to envision as you establish a new behavior. For example, to overcome her obstacle of discounting how much she deserved to be paid, an executive negotiating a higher salary envisioned a snowplow paving the way for her future and the future of other women.
- Share what you're learning with others so you can support each other.
- Create a short video to remind you of your desire and determination.
- Use a zero-tolerance focus word. For example, when I was working on this book, I knew things would get in the way. But if the word *book* was on my calendar, there was zero negotiation.

Becoming BullyProof is a process with wins and setbacks. Also, this journey isn't just about you; it's also about the other aspects of VBP: others, organizations, and society. Even if you become BullyProof, it takes work to stay that way and adapt to new challenges and situations.

If you'd like a way to track your progress, below is a quiz that will help you gain some insight about whether you are on the right path and how you can focus on leveraging your own growth to becoming BullyProof to help others.

BullyProof Quiz

For the following items, please indicate the degree to which they describe you by using the following scale:

1: not at all, 2: a little bit, 3: neutral, 4: somewhat, 5: very much

Self

1. I have healthy relationships with alphas.
2. I am confident in my ability to influence people.
3. I take the time to map out HOW I will achieve what I want.
4. I intentionally work on my BullyProof brand.
5. I have a response prepared to leverage either overt or Subtle Strength if someone attempts to dominate me.

Others

1. I am able to determine what type of alpha someone is.
2. I take time to support others in their ambitions.
3. I am invested in helping people help themselves.
4. I leverage overt or Subtle Strength to influence people.
5. I take the time to understand other people's challenges.

Organization

1. I act in alignment with my organization's values.
2. I spend time helping my organization navigate challenges.
3. I take action when someone is bullying in my organization.
4. I am invested in contributing to a positive work environment.
5. I advocate for mentoring at my organization.

Society

1. I build alliances outside of my organization.
2. I participate in causes that that help the greater good.
3. I advocate for underserved populations.
4. When I have power, I use it for good.
5. I work toward gaining VBP so I can help others.

Add up your total score for each area. If you score a 20 or higher in any group, you are leveraging that facet of VBP towards being BullyProof. In total, if you scored 80 or higher, you are well on your way to being BullyProof.

If you score less than 20 in any area, or lower than 80 overall, go back and look at which aspects of Value-Based Power you scored lowest on. This will give you an idea of where to focus next.

BullyProof Strategy #11: Finish with HOW

1. Choose one BullyProof behavior you want to build.
2. Write down the what, why, and when.
3. Write down the HOW: your habits, obstacles, and way forward.
4. Write down the who.
5. Take the BullyProof Quiz regularly to measure your progress.

OUR NEXT CHAPTER

Where Will We Grow Next?

The journey of writing this book started with a conversation with my daughter Reese. Reese often picks up my first book and asks me to read the part where I thank her mom and mention how special she is. She was so excited at the idea of writing a book and having her mommy's name in it. I asked Reese if there was anything she wanted to share in this book.

She said, "Let people know how we started writing together."

At first I thought, "Well, that line isn't going to lead to a bestseller." Then I thought about the deeper meaning. What she was most proud of was sitting together in my office and writing together as we listened to music and wrote notes on index cards. In that moment, my daughter taught me how important it was to pay attention to what is in front of me rather than worrying about what I had to get done that day. It was a great reminder of how simple things like being present can have a lasting impact. I can only hope my girls grow up being BullyProof and helping others along the way.

I know I am fortunate to interact and learn from executives around the world. A big part of my becoming BullyProof has been focusing more attention on practicing Value-Based Power and, in particular, strengthening society. Americans are very ambitious and resilient, and I love that about our culture. Where I see we can do more is increasing our balance and our emphasis on improving systems regardless of our political views.

We are going to have no shortage of controversies, crises, hardships, and good times. I consistently work to avoid getting pulled into bully bubbles. The traps are all around us. The media is brilliant at grabbing our attention and shifting it toward yet another shiny object. Being BullyProof means having good judgment but not being judgmental. As you saw in chapter 3, our minds are very powerful, and if we are intentional, we can increase the probability of positive experiences and decrease the probability of negative and reactive experiences.

We often forget that many of us want the same things, and we tend to get caught up in win/lose mindsets. I have been in far too many conversations where no one is listening to one another; they are just trying to convince others of why they are right. I believe that if each of us holds ourselves to a standard where we embrace a BullyProof mindset and engage in Value-Based Power, we will build more bridges than moats.

The more we work together to strengthen ourselves and society, the more negativity and wasted energy we take out of the system. This task is not a huge one: one conversation, one interaction, one intentional action can shape someone's day, year, career, or life.

Every day I try to focus on and build the foundational pillars of growth and strength. I try to work on myself daily and learn from those around me. Throughout the book I have shared interviews and insights from many of those people—those I admire and have learned from.

All through our lives we will come across people who will move us toward becoming BullyProof and people who will try to pull us away from becoming BullyProof. It is often the people who naturally exemplify Value-Based Power who will help us become BullyProof. As I mentioned, I struggled early in my life with being anxious, having a lack of confidence, and not having a voice. I let fear control what challenges I took on, and, in turn, I was neither a strong ally nor an advocate for others. I knew I wanted to find a way to turn this around, but I didn't know how. Fortunately, something clicked in my early college years.

Prior to transferring to Penn State, I attended Pace University, a small business school in New York. There I met lifelong friends who were from New York City and the Metro area nearby. There I did something I never thought I would do: I joined a fraternity, Delta Upsilon. While I am aware there are many challenges with fraternities, my experience there and the bonds I made changed my life and career for the better. Our fraternity's values included the advancement of justice, the promotion of friendship, the development of character, and the diffusion of liberal culture. I don't know for sure, but my sense is that these values helped me evolve into someone who believes strongly in Value-Based Power, being a leader, and public service.

What I learned from many of my fraternity brothers was the importance of standing up for yourself, advocating for what you believe in, and being loyal. Jeff Garbutt was one of those people. Jeff is now a retired NYPD sergeant and has seen the best and the worst in people. Jeff isn't shy about crediting himself as the person who helped me find my voice and the value of pushing through discomfort when it can help you succeed or help someone in need. Currently Jeff continues leveraging his Value-Based Power through his business, Prime Loyalty, where he brokers domains for businesses and people. What's different about Jeff's approach is he always focuses on others, organizations, and society first.

I share this story with you to offer some hope and inspiration. Even if you don't feel BullyProof today, you can be BullyProof tomorrow with a little help from others. It's important to have friends and colleagues in our lives with strong People and Purpose motivators because they naturally want to play a role in our ambitions and happiness.

Thank you for taking this journey with me. I cannot promise that you won't face people you won't be able to influence or who may make your life stressful. What I can promise you is that if you put the principles of BullyProof into practice, build alliances, advocate for others, and intentionally help yourself, others, organizations, and society, you will have many more wins than losses. I, for one, often catch myself getting pulled into a reactive state where I want to dominate or avoid people and situations. Every time I am able to hit the pause button and be intentional while using Subtle Strength, I consider it a small win that puts me in a stronger place to help others win.

On your BullyProof journey, you will open many doors for yourself. As you do, I invite you to hold the door for others.

ACKNOWLEDGMENTS

Writing a book is a team sport, and I am grateful for all the people who have supported my dreams. Thank you to my family—Reese, Rae, Keli, and our adopted Great Dane Cannoli—for providing a focus outside of the book and constant comic relief. The little things like watching the 9ers and Mets with my ladies gave me something to look forward to during writing sprints.

My smarter half, Dr. Keli Fazio, who is the chair of the Communication Department at TCNJ, was a force for making this book stronger and have more depth. She always helps me do my best to help people be their best. She spent countless hours helping me design surveys, ask questions, and challenging me to evolve my thinking. Sometimes it worked, and sometimes I didn't take the advice and rolled through the stop sign.

COVID-19 provided us some tough times that called for critical measures, such as getting a break from talking about masks and having some fun. Mike Archer of Janney Montgomery Scott was always willing to get out and play a round and talk about how natural my swing is as if I was born to golf. Funny, he kept yelling, "Fore!" after I hit my drives. He'd want me to let readers know that his cousin AJ Hewiston got a hole in one this year and Mike came up just a bit short.

When indoor gyms were closed and I wasn't able to get my workout fix, Lainey Gallagher of Haddonfield Fitness created outdoor fitness spaces and kept me going. She is the only reason I don't have to throw out all of my suits. Lainey also has great advice on the mental side of things, such as staying hydrated and relaxed.

Another group of friends that helped me recharge and enjoy some buddy time, including going to a Phil Collins concert, is our Haddonfield crew: Alex Phillips, Gary Wnek, and Greg Gudis. When I told them about the book and its topic around a firepit, their advice was "Let people in power know if someone is a jerk, don't give them power." Pretty sound advice to live by.

I appreciate the support from my mom, my sister Lauren, and my in-laws Geri and Dave Steuber. There were plenty of times they helped out with the kiddos so Keli and I could work.

I wouldn't have been able to learn about influence or deepen my understanding of alphas if it weren't for the people who believed in me and allowed me to work in their organizations. Sandra Martinez of Barnes has been a professional among professionals and has taught me how diversity, equity, and inclusion needs to be part of our daily decisions and actions.

We all need professional homes, and I found one in the Society of Consulting Psychology. Many people have mentored and guided me over the years. Dr. Steve Kincaid of gHSmart has been a positive influence on my consulting career since I started out and attended the Society of Consulting Psychology Midwinter Conference. Steve oozes credibility and has always been willing to help me learn. He was the first person to teach me about alpha personalities and how they test the people they interact with. Dr. Greg Pennington has shown me the importance of having important conversations around diversity and bringing people together. Dr. Ken Nowak is always willing to help and have a conversation. He introduced me to concepts and research in neuroscience that helped me think about the connection of neuroscience and influence. We all need thought partners and people we trust to be candid. Dr. Melanie Kinser of ThinkWyn has coached me through countless situations and is a true friend and often influences my thinking.

I am grateful for the guidance, kindness, and expertise from Corrine Moulder of Smith Publicity. If it weren't for her, I would not have gotten connected to Morgan James Publishing. It took me over three years and over thirty nos to get the yes I wanted. Bethany Marshall of Morgan James is an incredible thought partner and takes the time to understand what an author wants and how to make it happen.

Conversations lead to creativity, learning, and inspiration for me when I write. The more I learn, the more I can share. When I wanted to learn more about private equity firms and how to work with highly driven professionals, I reached out to Howard Ross of LLR Partners. Howard has spent countless hours answering my questions and helping me become better at influencing people who are top of their game. Scotty Boyarsky has become a great friend over the years and continues to be a solid sounding board and someone who gets it when it comes to leadership. Conversations with Martin Naylor about tough personalities and influence stuck with me as I thought through how to best help people equip themselves.

Much of what I do in business and the nonprofit world would not be possible without the inspiration and presence of Dr. Micah McCreary. His warmth and kindness is so important to our family that we gave our daughter Rae Micah his name.

Thank you to Michele Nunes and Neil Cavuto, who have spent years helping me get the word out to help people help themselves.

Scott Gardiner, president at Hire Vine, has been a force for staying positive in tough times and believing in the power of discipline. He helped me stay true to the importance of integrating challenges outside of work to keep my mind and focus fresh.

When I started on this adventure four years ago, Emily Turner and Joe Mangini were kind enough to sit with me and talk through what would make an impactful book. I am grateful for their insights and encouraging me to get something out there that will make a difference.

Amanda Rooker of Split Seed Media is the best editor and thought partner I have ever worked with. She brought the book to a level I never could have on my own and her drive to deliver so we can help people help themselves was a foundation for every conversation. I am grateful Amanda encouraged me to integrate the work of Dr. Danny Friedland and his research on the reactive and creative brain. Danny has recently passed, but his passion and work will live on for an eternity.

Creating the best possible images and tables to illustrate a point isn't as easy as I thought. Thank you to Ben Rooker of Split Seed Media, who was willing to take the time to understand what I wanted to accomplish and delivered. His expertise and professionalism made this a better book.

I am grateful for people like Grant Stinchfield, who believes my work needs to be out there more than I do. He challenges me to share my point of view and engage people.

Dr. Jim Burke has encouraged me since my early years in graduate school to get my work out there. He also inspired me to make this book better than my last one. Here's hoping I did.

And finally, to everyone I witnessed get bullied, dominated, or pushed around. You have inspired and will always inspire me to inspire you. Let's get BullyProof and pass it along.

ABOUT THE AUTHOR

Dr. Rob Fazio is the Managing Partner at OnPoint Advising, specializing in global leadership and organizational success. His approach to advising combines original research on power, influence, conversations, and motivation as well as over twenty years of consulting to elite performers. During the COVID-19 crisis, Rob advised hospitals and conducted presentations on Growth Leadership in times of crisis to support front-line health professionals and executive leadership. His work on flattening the anxiety curve has been featured on Fox News and in *The Hill*.

Based on his experiences in sport psychology and executive development, he teaches clients how to remove barriers to function at optimal levels. He has worked with executive teams and coached executives throughout organizations, including C-suites, surgeons, and emerging leaders.

Rob has contributed to *Forbes*, NBC News, *New York Daily News*, *HER Magazine*, *CEO Magazine*, *Philadelphia Business Journal*, and the American Management Association. His advice on navigating turbulent times and politics has been featured in the *New York Times* and on CNN, Fox News, MSNBC, and local networks.

His first book, *Simple Is the New Smart* (foreword by Neil Cavuto), features success strategies he gleaned from over a decade and a half of working with athletes, executives, and people driven toward excellence.

Recently he developed the Motivational Currency® Calculator. This self-assessment reveals what drives people, how well someone can read another person's motivators, and how effective someone is at using the best approach to tap into someone's motivators.

He has developed significant expertise in advising Fortune 500 organizations globally in developing, advising, and retaining employees based on a future-oriented strategy, organizational values, culture, and person/position fit. He has worked internationally in a variety of industries, including finance/banking, private equity, accounting, media, pharmaceuticals, hospitals, telecommunications, chemicals, retail, sports, public utilities, and nonprofits. Rob is often asked to be a keynote speaker or facilitator at executive off-sites.

Rob has served as a performance excellence consultant to a variety of organizations and athletic teams. He participated in the development and facilitation of the life-skills portion of the NFL's Coaching Academy and the PGA's 1st Tee programs.

He is the founder and president of a September 11–inspired nonprofit organization, Hold the Door for Others (HoldtheDoor. com). The organization's mission is to challenge and equip people to grow through loss and adversity and achieve their dreams.

Prior to starting OnPoint Advising, he worked at Leadership Research Institute and Hay Group. Rob completed his BA in psychology at The Pennsylvania State University. He earned an MEd in athletic counseling from Springfield College and an MS and

PhD in counseling psychology with a subspeciality in performance consulting from Virginia Commonwealth University. Rob completed his clinical rotation at the University of Pennsylvania. Rob is a licensed psychologist in the state of Pennsylvania. He lives just outside Philadelphia in Haddonfield, New Jersey, with his wife Keli, daughters Reese and Rae, and adopted Great Dane Cannoli.

FURTHER RESOURCES

You can stay connected to all things BullyProof and download free tools and resources at https://onpointadvising.com/bullyproof/.

In addition, for our most up-to-date resources and Bully-Proof strategies, please join the GetOnPoint newsletter at https://onpointadvising.com/onpoint-newsletter/, visit our video blog at https://onpointadvising.com/video-blog/, and visit out insights page at https://onpointadvising.com/insights/.

Follow Rob on LinkedIn for up-to-date microlearning videos and tips on leadership and becoming BullyProof.

To book Rob for a keynote, please visit https://onpointadvising.com/keynote-speaker/.

ENDNOTES

1   Workplace Bullying Institute and Zogby Analytics, *2021 WBI U.S. Workplace Bullying Survey: The Fifth National Scientific WBI Study*, 2021, https://workplacebullying.org/wp-content/uploads/2021/04/2021-Full-Report.pdf.

2   Kenneth M. Nowack, "Toxic Bosses May Cause Health Risk," *Talent Management* (January/February 2016): 29, 56; "Bullying in the Workplace," OSH Answers Fact Sheets, https://www.ccohs.ca/oshanswers/psychosocial/bullying.html, cited in Sherri Gordon, "The Effects of Workplace Bullying," Verywell Mind, March 10, 2020, https://www.verywellmind.com/what-are-the-effects-of-workplace-bullying-460628#citation-1.

3   Sherri Gordon, "Workplace Bullying Causes Anxiety Issues," Verywell Mind, August 22, 2021, https://www.verywellmind.com/workplace-bullying-causes-anxiety-issues-460629; and Morten Birkeland Nielsen, Nils Magerøy, Johannes Gjerstad, and Ståle Einarsen, "Workplace Bullying and Subsequent Health Problems," *Tidsskr Nor Laegeforen* 134 (July 2014): 1233–1238, https://doi.org/10.4045/tidsskr.13.0880.

4   Tea Lallukka et al., "Workplace Bullying and Subsequent Psychotropic Medication: A Cohort Study with Register Linkag-

es," *BMJ Open* 2, no. 6 (2012), https://doi.org/10.1136/bm-jopen-2012-001660, cited in Gordon, "Effects of Workplace Bullying."

5 Erika L. Sabbath et al. , "Mental Health Expenditures: Association with Workplace Incivility and Bullying among Hospital Patient Care Workers," *Journal of Occupational and Environmental Medicine* 60, no. 8 (August 2018): 737–742, https://doi.org/10.1097/JOM.0000000000001322; and Erika L. Sabbath et al., "Cohort Profile: The Boston Hospital Workers Health Study (BHWHS)," *International Journal of Epidemiology* 47, no. 6 (December 2018): 1739–1740g, https://doi.org/10.1093/ije/dyy164, as cited in Katherine J. Igoe, "It's Not Just Personal: The Economic Value of Preventing Bullying in the Workplace," *Harvard University T.H. Chan School of Public Health*, March 4, 2020, https://www.hsph.harvard.edu/ecpe/economic-value-preventing-workplace-bullying/.

6 Gordon, "Effects of Workplace Bullying."

7 WBI and Zogby, *2021 WBI U.S. Workplace Bullying Survey*.

8 Alex Miller, "Understanding the Costs of Harassment Prevention and DEI Training," *American Bar Association*, May 14, 2021, https://www.americanbar.org/groups/business_law/publications/blt/2021/05/harassment-prevention.

9 Igoe, "It's Not Just Personal"; Ståle Einarsen et al., "Climate for Conflict Management, Exposure to Workplace Bullying and Work Engagement: A Moderated Mediation Analysis," *International Journal of Human Resource Management* 29, no. 3 (2018): 549–570, https://doi.org/10.1080/09585192.2016.1164216; and David Sparkman, "The True Costs of Workplace Bullying," EHS Today, June 22, 2020, https://

www.ehstoday.com/workplace-bullying/article/21134760/
the-true-costs-of-workplace-bullying.

10 Robert I. Sutton, *The No A$$hole Rule: Building a Civilized Workplace and Surviving One That Isn't* (New York: Business Plus, 2007).

11 For more information about the victim cycle, the ownership cycle, and the Pathway to Ownership, see Rob Fazio, *Simple Is the New Smart* (Newburyport, MA: Career Press, 2016).

12 "Narcissistic Personality Disorder," WebMD, June 18, 2020, https://www.webmd.com/mental-health/narcissistic-personality-disorder.

13 "DSM-IV and DSM-5 Criteria for the Personality Disorders," American Psychiatric Association, accessed October 16, 2021, https://www.nyu.edu/gsas/dept/philo/courses/materials/Narc. Pers.DSM.pdf.

14 This section is summarized from Daniel Friedland, *Living Well from Within: A Neuroscience and Mindfulness-Based Framework for Conscious Leadership* (San Diego: SuperSmartHealth, 2016), chapters 2, 5, and 6.

15 Kelly McGonigal, *Upside of Stress: Why Stress Is Good for You, and How You Can Get Good at It* (New York: Avery, 2015), xxi, cited in Friedland, *Living Well from Within*, 58.

16 Friedland, *Living Well from Within*, 142.

17 Ibid.

18 Richard E. Boyatzis and Anthony I. Jack, "The Neuroscience of Coaching," *Consulting Psychology Journal: Practice and Research* 70, no. 1 (2018): 11–27, https://doi.org/10.1037/cpb0000095.

19 Anthony I. Jack et al., "Visioning in the Brain: An fMRI Study of Inspirational Coaching and Mentoring," *Social Neuroscience* 8, no. 4 (2013): 369–384, https://doi.org/10.1

080/17470919.2013.808259.

20 Paul J. Zak, "The Neuroscience of High-Trust Organizations," *Consulting Psychology Journal: Practice and Research* 70, no. 1 (2018): 45–58, https://doi.org/10.1037/cpb0000076.

21 Ibid.

22 Ibid.

23 Jordan Harbinger, "Episode 16: Tali Sharot: Unpacking the Science of the Influential Mind," The Jordan Harbinger Show podcast, accessed December 2, 2021, https://www.jordanharbinger.com/tali-sharot-unpacking-the-science-of-the-influential-mind/.

24 Ibid. See also Tali Sharot, *The Influential Mind: What the Brain Reveals About our Power to Change Others* (New York: Henry Holt, 2017).

25 Wray Herbert, *On Second Thought: Outsmarting Your Mind's Hard-Wired Habits* (New York: Crown, 2010); and Daniel Kahneman, *Thinking, Fast and Slow* (New York: Farrar, Straus and Giroux, 2013).

26 Herbert, *On Second Thought.*

27 "Gender Bias," APA Dictionary of Psychology, accessed December 4, 2021, https://dictionary.apa.org/gender-bias.

28 Ibid.

29 Bulleted list is directly quoted from Kenneth Nowack and Dan Radecki, "Introduction to the Special Issue: Neuro-Mythconceptions in Consulting Psychology—between a Rock and a Hard Place," *Consulting Psychology Journal: Practice and Research* 70, no. 1 (2018): 1–10, http://dx.doi.org/10.1037/cpb0000108.

30 Robert Eichenger, keynote presentation, Society of Consulting Psychology, Seattle, WA, February 10, 2017.

31 K. Anders Ericsson, Michael J. Prietula, and Edward T. Coke-

ly, "The Making of an Expert," *Harvard Business Review*, July-August 2007, https://hbr.org/2007/07/the-making-of-an-expert.

32 Ibid.

33 Thanks to thought leader Gagandeep Singh for identifying these different types of motivation theories.

34 David C. McClelland, *Human Motivation* (Northbrook, IL: Scott Foresman, 1983).

35 Rob Fazio, "Pay People with Their Motivational Currency" *The CEO Magazine*, March 11, 2016, http://media. the-ceo-magazine.com/guest/pay-people-their-motivational-currency.

36 To learn more about the business case for EI, a good place to start is the EI Consortium at www.eiconsortium.org.

37 Rob Fazio, *Simple Is the New Smart* (Newburyport, MA: Career Press, 2016),169–180.

38 Aon, *Global Risk Management Survey*, 2017, https://www. aon.com/2017-global-risk-management-survey/pdfs/2017-Aon-Global-Risk-Management-Survey-Full-Report-062617. pdf.

39 World Health Organization, "Investing in Treatment for Depression and Anxiety Leads to Fourfold Return," news release, April 13, 2016, https://www.who.int/news/item/13-04-2016-investing-in-treatment-for-depression-and-anxiety-leads-to-fourfold-return.

40 Paragraph adapted from Rob Fazio, "Preparing Leaders to Be Ahead of the Curve: The Successful 7 Reopening Resources for after the COVID-19 Crisis," *CEO World*, April 29, 2020, https://ceoworld.biz/2020/04/29/preparing-leaders-to-be-ahead-of-the-curve/.

41 Viktor E. Frankl, "The Case for Tragic Optimism," in *Man's*

Search for Meaning (Boston: Beacon Press, 2006).

42 Lawrence G. Calhoun and Richard G. Tedeschi, *Handbook of Posttraumatic Growth: Research and Practice* (Oxfordshire, UK: Taylor & Francis, 2014); Robert J. Fazio, "Growth Consulting: Practical Methods of Facilitating Growth through Loss and Adversity," *Journal of Clinical Psychology: In Session* 65, no. 5 (2009): 532–543, DOI: 10.1002/jclp.20590.

43 Gabriel Perna, "HSS CEO Lou Shapiro on Reallocating 85% of Resources to Battle COVID-19," Health Evolution, March 23, 2020, https://www.healthevolution.com/insider/hss-ceo-lou-shapiro-on-reallocating-85-of-resources-to-battle-covid-19/.

44 Ibid.

45 PwC, "Global Crisis Survey 2021," accessed December 4, 2021, https://www.pwc.com/gx/en/issues/crisis-solutions/global-crisis-survey.html.

46 American Bar Association, *A Current Glance at Women in the Law*, January 2018, https://www.pbi.org/docs/default-source/default-document-library/10569_a-current-glance-at-women-in-the-law-jan-2018-(1).pdf?sfvrsn=0, cited in "The Women's Leadership Gap: Women's Leadership by the Numbers," Center for American Progress, November 20, 2018, https://www.americanprogress.org/article/womens-leadership-gap-2/.

47 U.S. Bureau of Labor Statistics, "Labor Force Statistics from the Current Population Survey: Employed persons by detailed occupation, sex, race, and Hispanic or Latino ethnicity"; Association of American Medical Colleges, "Table 10: 2015 Benchmarking—Permanent and Interim Decanal Positions" (2016), https://www.aamc.org/download/481204/data/2015table10.pdf., cited in Center for American Progress,

"Women's Leadership Gap."

48 "U.S. Women Earned More PhDs Than Men Last Year," Statista, October 8, 2018, https://www.statista.com/ chart/15685/doctoral-degrees-awarded-by-broad-field-and-gender-in-the-us/; and Heather L. Johnson, "Pipelines, Pathways, and Institutional Leadership: An Update on the Status of Women in Higher Education" (Washington, DC: American Council on Education's Center for Policy Research and Strategy, 2017), https://www.acenet.edu/news-room/ Documents/HES-Pipelines-Pathways-and-Institutional-Leadership-2017.pdf., cited in Center for American Progress, "Women's Leadership Gap."

49 "Women in Financial Services," Catalyst, June 29, 2020, https://www.catalyst.org/knowledge/women-financial-services; and Claire Zillman, "With First Woman CFO Dhivya Suryadevara, GM Enters Rare Fortune 500 Territory," *Fortune*, June 14, 2018, http://fortune.com/2018/06/14/dhivya-suryadevara-gm-cfo/., cited in Center for American Progress, "Women's Leadership Gap."

50 Anne Stych, "Percentage of Women CEOs Rises during Challenging Business Year," *BizWomen*, January 4, 2021, https:// www.bizjournals.com/bizwomen/news/latest-news/2021/01/ percentage-of-women-ceos-rises-during-challenging.html?page=all; and Center for American Progress, "Women's Leadership Gap."

51 Pragya Agarwal, "Are Women and Men Being Treated the Same in the Workplace?" *Forbes*, March 3, 2020, https:// www.forbes.com/sites/pragyaagarwaleurope/2020/03/03/are-women-and-men-being-treated-the-same-in-the-workplace/.

52 Sally Helgesen and Marshall Goldsmith, *How Women Rise: Break the 12 Habits Holding You Back from Your Next*

Raise, Promotion, or Job (New York: Hachette, 2018).

53 Hugh Son, "Goldman Won't Take Companies Public without 'At Least One Diverse Board Candidate,' CEO Says," CNBC, January 23, 2020, https://www.cnbc.com/2020/01/23/goldman-wont-take-companies-public-that-dont-have-at-least-one-diverse-board-candidate-ceo-says.html.

54 "Nasdaq to Advance Diversity through New Proposed Listing Requirements," Nasdaq, December 1, 2020, https://www.nasdaq.com/press-release/nasdaq-to-advance-diversity-through-new-proposed-listing-requirements-2020-12-01.

55 Kate Ludeman and Eddie Erlandson, "Coaching the Alpha Male," *Harvard Business Review*, May 2004, https://hbr.org/2004/05/coaching-the-alpha-male.

56 These two sections are adapted from Rob Fazio, "The Importance of the Alpha Female," *Forbes*, March 9, 2020, https://www.forbes.com/sites/forbescoachescouncil/2020/03/09/the-importance-of-the-alpha-female/?sh=59692c791905.

57 "New Research Shows Women Are Better at Using Soft Skills Crucial for Effective Leadership and Superior Business Performance, Finds Korn Ferry," *Korn Ferry*, March 7, 2016, https://www.kornferry.com/about-us/press/new-research-shows-women-are-better-at-using-soft-skills-crucial-for-effective-leadership.

58 Carol Kinsey Goman, "Is Your Communication Style Dictated by Your Gender?" *Forbes*, March 31, 2016, https://www.forbes.com/sites/carolkinseygoman/2016/03/31/is-your-communication-style-dictated-by-your-gender/?sh=138de554eb9d.

59 Uri Friedman, "New Zealand's Prime Minister May Be the Most Effective Leader on the Planet," *The Atlantic*, April 19, 2020, https://www.theatlantic.com/politics/archive/2020/04/

jacinda-ardern-new-zealand-leadership-coronavirus/610237/;
and Tess McClure, "Jacinda Ardern's Popularity Plunges as
New Zealand Reckons with New Era of Endemic Covid," *The
Guardian*, November 10, 2021, https://www.theguardian.
com/world/2021/nov/11/jacinda-arderns-popularity-plung-
es-as-new-zealand-reckons-with-new-era-of-endemic-covid.

60 Fazio, "Importance of the Alpha Female."

61 Helgesen and Goldsmith, *How Women Rise*.

62 Henri Tajfel, "Experiments in Intergroup Discrimination," *Scientific American* 223, no. 5 (1970): 96–102, http://
doi.org/10.1038/scientificamerican1170-96.

63 Jay J. Van Bavel and Andrea Pereira, "The Partisan Brain:
An Identity-Based Model of Political Belief," *Trends in
Cognitive Sciences* 22, no. 3 (2018): 213–224, https://
doi.org/10.1016/j.tics.2018.01.004. See David McRaney,
"YANSS 171: How Partisan Identities Affect Our Ability to Reason, Rationalize, and Recall," You Are Not So
Smart podcast, January 29, 2020, https://youarenotsosmart.
com/2020/01/29/yanss-171-how-partisan-identities-af-
fect-our-ability-to-reason-rationalize-and-recall/.

64 Taijfel, "Experiments in Intergroup Discrimination."

65 Van Bavel and Pereira, "The Partisan Brain."

66 McRaney, "YANSS 171: Partisan Identities."

67 Van Bavel and Pereira, "The Partisan Brain."

68 Jay Van Bavel, "Do Politics Make Us Irrational?" TED-Ed,
February 2020, https://www.ted.com/talks/jay_van_bavel_
do_politics_make_us_irrational/transcript#t-69437.

69 Ibid.

70 Van Bavel and Pereira, "The Partisan Brain," 8.

71 Van Bavel and Pereira, "The Partisan Brain," 9.

72 Laura Morgan Roberts and Anthony J. Mayo, "Toward a

Racially Just Workplace," *Harvard Business Review*, November 14, 2019, https://hbr.org/2019/11/toward-a-racially-just-workplace.

73 Andrés Tapia, "The Latino Leadership Shortage," *Korn Ferry*, accessed November 30, 2021, https://www.kornferry.com/insights/this-week-in-leadership/latino-leadership-shortage-autentico.

74 "QuickFacts: United States," United States Census Bureau, accessed December 4, 2021, https://www.census.gov/quickfacts/fact/table/US/LFE046219; Anne Stych, "Percentage of Women CEOs Rises during Challenging Business Year," *BizWomen*, January 4, 2021, https://www.bizjournals.com/bizwomen/news/latest-news/2021/01/percentage-of-women-ceos-rises-during-challenging.html?page=all, accessed December 4, 2021; and "The Women's Leadership Gap: Women's Leadership by the Numbers," Center for American Progress, November 20, 2018, https://www.americanprogress.org/article/womens-leadership-gap-2/.

75 Cary Funk and Kim Parker, "4. Blacks in STEM Jobs Are Especially Concerned about Diversity and Discrimination in the Workplace," Pew Research Center, January 9, 2018, https://www.pewresearch.org/social-trends/2018/01/09/blacks-in-stem-jobs-are-especially-concerned-about-diversity-and-discrimination-in-the-workplace/.

76 Praveen Shrestha, "Ebbinghaus Forgetting Curve," Psychestudy, November 17, 2017, https://www.psychestudy.com/cognitive/memory/ebbinghaus-forgetting-curve.

77 Lien B. Pham and Shelley E. Taylor, "From Thought to Action: Effects of Process- Versus Outcome-Based Mental Simulations on Performance," *Personality and Social Psychology Bulletin* 25, no. 2 (1999): 250-260, doi:10.1177/014616729

9025002010.

78 Tali Sharot, "The Optimism Bias," TED Talk, February 2012, https://www.ted.com/talks/tali_sharot_the_optimism_bias?language=en.

79 Gabriele Oettingen, *Rethinking Positive Thinking: Inside the New Science of Motivation* (Current, 2015); and "The Science behind WOOP," WOOP website, https://woopmylife.org/en/science.

80 Julian Linden, "Coach Reveals Tricks He Used to Prepare Phelps," Reuters, August 20, 2008, https://www.reuters.com/article/us-olympics-swimming-phelps/coach-reveals-tricks-he-used-to-prepare-phelps-idUSSP27658220080820; and Childs Walker, "A Grown-Up Michael Phelps Looks Back on the Beijing Olympics, 10 Years Later," *The Baltimore Sun*, August 10, 2018, https://www.baltimoresun.com/sports/olympics/bs-sp-michael-phelps-beijing-anniversary-0812-htmlstory.html.

81 Laura K. Globig, Kristin Witte, Gloria Feng, and Tali Sharot, "Under Threat, Weaker Evidence Is Required to Reach Undesirable Conclusions," *Journal of Neuroscience* 41, no. 30 (2021): 6502-6510, DOI: https://doi.org/10.1523/JNEUROSCI.3194-20.2021.

A free ebook edition is available with the purchase of this book.

To claim your free ebook edition:

1. Visit MorganJamesBOGO.com
2. Sign your name CLEARLY in the space
3. Complete the form and submit a photo of the entire copyright page
4. You or your friend can download the ebook to your preferred device

Morgan James BOGO™

A **FREE** ebook edition is available for you or a friend with the purchase of this print book.

CLEARLY SIGN YOUR NAME ABOVE

Instructions to claim your free ebook edition:
1. Visit MorganJamesBOGO.com
2. Sign your name CLEARLY in the space above
3. Complete the form and submit a photo of this entire page
4. You or your friend can download the ebook to your preferred device

Print & Digital Together Forever.

Snap a photo

Free ebook

Read anywhere

CPSIA information can be obtained
at www.ICGtesting.com
Printed in the USA
JSHW081104111022
31538JS00001B/23